soul train

The Music, Dance, and Style of a Generation

QUESTLOVE

Harper Design
An Imprint of HarperCollins Publishers
An Insight Editions Book

All photos are courtesy of Soul Train Holdings, LLC. Special thank-yous to the Soul Train team: Kenard Gibbs, Kim Porter Fluellen, and Donna Schaffer.

Text copyright © 2013 by Ahmir-Khalib Thompson
Foreword copyright © 2013 by Gladys Knight
Preface copyright © 2013 by Nick Cannon
Photographs copyright © 2013 by Soul Train Holdings, LLC
Interior design and layout: Rachel Maloney

All rights reserved. No part of this book may be used or reproduced in any manner whatsoever without written permission except in the case of brief quotations embodied in critical articles and reviews. For information, address Harper Design, 10 East 53rd Street, New York, NY 10022.

Published in 2013 by:
Harper Design
An Imprint of HarperCollins Publishers
10 East 53rd Street
New York, NY 10022
Tel (212) 207-7000
harperdesign@harpercollins.com
www.harpercollins.com

Distributed throughout the world by:
HarperCollinsPublishers
10 East 53rd Street
New York, NY 10022

Produced by

10 Paul Drive
San Rafael, CA 94912
www.insighteditions.com

Insight Editions would like to especially thank Kenard Gibbs, Partner and CEO of Soul Train Holdings, LLC; Kim Porter Fluellen, Vice President, Integrated Marketing of Soul Train Holdings, LLC; and Donna Schaffer, curator extraordinaire and long-time *Soul Train* expert. Also, a special thank you to Questlove for his commitment to telling the world about the importance of the *Soul Train* legacy.

Library of Congress Control Number: 2013940639

ISBN: 978-0-06-228838-7

Printed in Hong Kong

First printing, 2013

OPPOSITE: Don dancing in Episode 396 on June 26, 1982. **PAGES 8-9:** A classic scene featuring dancers Pat Davis and Damita Jo Freeman.

Contents

Foreword by Gladys Knight • 10
Preface by Nick Cannon • 12
Introduction: Laying Down the Tracks • 14

Part 1
Love—The 1970s • 21

The Big Idea • 23
A Small Start for a Big Idea • Leavin' on a Morning Train to California •
Al Green • The First Family of Soul (Train) •
The Ubiquitous Jacksons

The Acts • 49
Stevie Wonder • Marvin Gaye • Rock Royalty Sink or Swim •
Motown and *Soul Train* • Jazzin' Up *Soul Train* •
Appealing to a New Generation • Tribute to James Brown •
Funk Fever • The Supergroup Sensation • Cash Chameleons •
Disco: A Brief Derailing? Or a Change with the Times?

The Moves • 91
Season 1 Dancers • The *Soul Train* Line •
Spotlight on Damita Jo • High Energy •
From Street to *Saturday Night Fever* • Stepping Out of Line •
Focus on Fashion • Spotlight on Jeffrey and Jody

The Big Moments • 107
The O'Jays • The Fifth Beatle • The Isley Brothers •
Average White Band and the Undisputed Truth •
Trifecta • Elton John • David Bowie •
The End of the Decade

Part 2
Peace—The 1980s • 119

The Idea • 121
Kicking and Screaming • Tribute to Smokey Robinson •
Keep Moving or Die • A New Genre and a New Jackson •
From Funk to Pop • Welcome Back to the Future:
Take One • Welcome Back to the Future: Take Two •
Hip-Hop as It Happened

The Acts • 147
The Boys Are Back in Town • A New Rubric •
Protégé Power: Punk Funk vs Purple Rock • Blue-Eyed Soul •
Expanding Horizons

The Moves • 165
Meet the Cast • Spotlight on Louie "Ski" Carr •
A Hip-Hop Skip and a Jump down the *Soul Train* Line

The Big Moments • 179
A Salute to Rick James • LL Cool J • Teddy Pendergrass •
Yarbrough & Peoples • The Pointer Sisters • Patti LaBelle •
A Salute to Jermaine Jackson • A Tribute to Marvin Gaye •
Soul Train Spectrum • Herbie Hancock • Kool & the Gang •
A Salute to Diana Ross • A Note About New Jack—and Don Dancing •
The Cult of Personality • The End of the Decade

Part 3
Soul—The 1990s • 199

The Idea • 201
Meditations on the Theme • The Decade-Defining Sound

The Acts • 209
Back to Beastie • Bell Biv DeVoe • Lenny Kravitz •
Alternative Black Music • Classic Collaboration

The Moves • 219
The Backup Moves Up Front • Meet the Cast

The Big Moments • 225
Tribute to Quincy Jones • Tribute to Stevie Wonder •
Tribute to Gladys Knight • Gerald and Eddie Levert •
Move to Movies • Introducing Girl Power •
Vision of Mariah • Turning the Corner

The End of the Road: Episode 734 • 234

Afterword: Unlocking the Treasure Trove • 238
Acknowledgments • 240

foreword
BY GLADYS KNIGHT

From my very first performance on *Soul Train* in 1971, I remember thinking that this innovative show was such an amazing platform to showcase so many artists' talents. I had been performing with the Pips for several years at that point, but there was nothing like performing on *Soul Train*. And the Pips and I were dreaming big dreams at that time. We wanted to be the best group in the world, and we wanted to entertain above everything else. *Soul Train* was a great stage for us.

Soul Train was such a welcoming venue for our craft, and that wouldn't have been possible without the ingenuity of Don Cornelius. God bless him for fighting against the social ills, such as racial prejudice, and for succeeding in getting so many talented black voices on national television. I feel truly honored to have known Don. He just had a way about him and he never ceased to amaze me.

I remember back when the Pips and I won our first Grammy. Of course, I knew I would be overwhelmed if we actually won, so I made sure to record the show at home to enjoy the moment later on. Soon after the show, I gathered everyone around in our living room to watch the tape, and, of course, the TV hadn't recorded anything from that night. I was so disappointed. I told Don this story and, what do you know, at our next appearance on *Soul Train*, he had our Grammy-winning moment on the big screen for us to watch. He was just so thoughtful like that.

Don succeeded with his vision for *Soul Train*, and he wanted to see everyone around him succeed as well. I'm happy to have walked that journey with him. He was a truly amazing man who encouraged all of us on the show to just be ourselves, which is why we danced the way we danced and talked the way we talked. He knew what he was doing, and he did it with ease and confidence. He was also always sure to let us know how proud of us he was. I'm so fortunate to have been a part of Don's *Soul Train* world.

OPPOSITE By Episode 97 in May 1974, Gladys Knight & the Pips had left Motown for Buddha Records, where they would continue making top-rated albums.

Preface
BY NICK CANNON

My earliest memories of *Soul Train* are of dancing in front of the TV as a toddler. My mom loves to tell those stories. When given the chance, I would choose *Soul Train* over cartoons. As I got older, I would see different dance moves take off after being showcased on *Soul Train*. It was an amazing vehicle for dance culture from its very early days. And it was a huge deal for me watching a lot of the dancers start on *Soul Train* and then, from there, begin to dance for a lot of the major artists of the day.

Soul Train acted as the music curator for the community, as all the new songs and new acts were introduced through the show. Dancing came first for me, but once I started getting into the music, I remember New Edition's memorable performance. It stood out in a big way for me, and they really set the tone for how *Soul Train* could evolve. And when the hip-hop acts started, that was big. Artists that I was hearing on my friends' boom boxes on the basketball courts and on the playground were brought to life through *Soul Train*. I remember seeing LL Cool J on TV and having a "wow" moment. I thought to myself, so that's what he looks like. He was a superstar to me.

As an avid fan, I experienced a dream come true with my first national TV appearance: dancing on *Soul Train* as a fifteen-year-old. I didn't meet the age requirement, but I managed to sneak in with a few ladies. (And I'd like to take this moment to thank all of those ladies who let me roll with them inside the *Soul Train* set.) Many times after that first performance, I made the two-hour drive to Hollywood to wait outside the *Soul Train* studio on the corner of Gower and Melrose. I was hooked from the beginning. I would always make sure to have on my best outfit, get a fresh haircut, and practice all of my dance moves so that I would be chosen. Not only did I love to dance, but I knew that appearing on *Soul Train* had the potential to be my entry into the Hollywood industry in a very real way. It was the only way that I had the opportunity to meet artists and people that were in Hollywood. As a young, aspiring entertainer, I knew *Soul Train* was a definite foot in the door.

Memories of *Soul Train* wouldn't be complete without remembering Don Cornelius. He was the epitome of showbiz. Don really represented the business aspect of it all. Not only was he in

front of the camera, but he was behind the scenes in all aspects as executive producer. Watching him on camera handling the artists made me think, "I want to do that." He definitely became a blueprint for a lot of the things I'm doing today. He showed the world what a music industry guy was and he opened the door for so many entertainers. We got closer as the years went on, and I would always remind him of back in the day when I was a nagging little kid trying to get a record deal from him. I wanted to seize the moment even though I didn't really know how things worked. I didn't know there were actually heads of record labels. To me, Don could do everything.

Soul Train is everlasting. It's done so much for our culture, and I believe in keeping the brand alive. It acts as a history book telling us how artists performed back then. We will always remember how Al Green, Marvin Gaye, Stevie Wonder, and the Jackson 5 did it, to name just a few. They paved the way for artists to take a chance and come into their own. As the necessary leaders, they laid the foundation for greatness. Their ideas and performances on the show allowed new artists to pick up the torch. *Soul Train* will continue to educate and inspire for many generations to come.

OPPOSITE The women dancers of the '80s.

Introduction
LAYING DOWN THE TRACKS

What is *Soul Train*? It's a television show, but it's not only a television show. It's a transformative cultural moment, but it's not only a transformative cultural moment. To me, at least, *Soul Train* was a sibling, a parent, a babysitter, a friend, a textbook, a newscast, a business school, and a church. Growing up in my house in Philadelphia in the '70s, we weren't allowed to watch anything on television except *Sesame Street* and *Soul Train.* It was already a house filled with music—my father had been a doo-wop star and was still performing in an act with my mother—but thanks to *Soul Train*, we also had the music of many other performers filling the house.

I was born in 1971, in January, and by 1973 I was already hearing the *Soul Train* theme, and seeing the *Soul Train* title moving across the screen. Music came from records, that much I knew, and I was obsessed with record labels, the actual circular labels. I used to spin them around in my hands, imagining what sounds they would make on the turntable—but music also came from the television. To this day, some of my formative memories are fused to certain performances, the way that certain scenes in movie history have their soundtrack irreversibly and permanently attached to them. An example: when I was about two, I came running out of the bathroom, fresh from a bath, still wet. I went straight to the living room, where I promptly slipped and skidded into a radiator. It sizzled against the water on my skin, but also against the skin itself. Until my teens, I had a burn there. It's not the kind of event you would forget even without a scar, but just as vivid as the sound of the radiator is what was playing on the TV: the Chicago soul legend Curtis Mayfield, wearing a long-sleeve shirt open at the collar, singing "Freddie's Dead." Let me focus in a little more, when I got burned, it was the section of the song about a minute and a half in where the horns enter. To me, that's one of the scariest moments in soul music, not because there's anything objectively frightening about it—though the horns are crying a bit—but because I associate it with the radiator.

It wasn't just memorable moments of Curtis, of course. It was everyone. My parents loved Bill Withers, but the appeal was abstract to me until I saw him, concretely, on the screen. I have mentioned how I was obsessed with record labels, but that was only the tip of my obsessive iceberg. When I heard a song, I tried to imagine everything about the artist: what they wore, how they held the microphone; whether they looked out into the audience or at other band members; whether they mostly stood in place (like Aretha Franklin) or moved in choreographed perfection (like the Jackson 5), or even sat down (like Sly Stone). Long before YouTube, long before MTV, it was much harder to complete the pictures of music in your mind. *Soul Train* made it all come clear. Week after week, hour after hour, you could see artists playing their own music, and not just playing it, but using it to make a real connection with their audience. *Soul Train* had early Al Green performances (in shorts, boots, and a hat, no less) and late Marvin Gaye ones (a tribute episode from 1983, just before his murder, that included a charming interview with Marvin's daughter Nona in which she identified her father as her favorite singer). *Soul Train* crammed Barry White's Love Unlimited Orchestra onto a cramped studio set. *Soul Train* showed Chaka Khan emerging as the new queen of soul. *Soul*

> *It's always a pleasure to find something that matters.*
>
> —Don Cornelius

14 | SOUL TRAIN

ABOVE When I watched *Soul Train* as a little kid, I could've sworn the Kids were looking directly at me, as if to say, "Welcome to the party."

Train passed the torch to New Edition, came out in (equivocal) support of rap pioneers like Run-D.M.C. and LL Cool J, and even extended an invitation to a funky little band called the Roots. Under the stable leadership and solid presence of Don Cornelius, the quintessential professional always donning shirts with firmly pressed lapels, *Soul Train* was the master of teaching you lessons that you didn't know you were being taught.

The *Soul Train* Effect

In 1971, when *Soul Train* was first syndicated, in just six cities, it was the first time that many people had ever seen black Americans at the center of an entertainment television show. The sixties brought tremendous changes to the American landscape, but television was still a largely white affair; trailblazers like Bill Cosby in *I Spy* and Diahann Carroll in *Julia* were conspicuous exceptions. When Don Cornelius blew the whistle and started the train, much of his motive came from a desire to counter the notion that black Americans were "buffoons or negative-looking people or people who are antisocial in any way." He did that, and more, for years on end. The *Soul Train* Kids revolutionized dance. His interviews were witty and intimate, and filled with mutual respect between him and the artists. And the show worked a kind of unifying magic at one of the most tense and uncertain times in African American history, with the murders of Martin Luther King Jr. and Robert Kennedy still painfully fresh and the fabric of American cities beginning to unravel.

The sense of affirmation was everywhere. In some ways, in fact, the music was only part of the *Soul Train* experience; just as important were the commercials, which were run by Johnson Products, the maker of Ultra Sheen and Afro Sheen hair products. The history of African American hair could fill another book, and probably has—black people believed they should be ashamed of their natural hair texture—but *Soul Train* ran ads that turned that mind-set on its head, urging that Afros were

LAYING DOWN THE TRACKS

ROLL CALL: SEASON 1

In just one season, Don transformed *Soul Train* from a six-city startup to a seventeen-city syndicate. It had everything to do with the lineup.

HEADLINERS:
Gladys Knight & the Pips
Charles Wright & the Watts
Chairman of the Board
The Staple Singers
Bill Withers
Lou Rawls
Martha and the Vandellas
Friends of Distinction
The Chambers Brothers
Junior Walker & the All Stars
Jean Knight
Chi-Lites
Gene Chandler
BB King
Dennis Coffey
Little Richard
Undisputed Truth
Curtis Mayfield
The Impressions
The Dells
Jerry Butler and Brenda Lee
Al Green
The Four Tops
Rufus Thomas
Wilson Pickett
Joe Tex

I had a burning desire to see black people presented on television in a positive light.

—Don Cornelius

ABOVE In the early '70s, *Soul Train* broadcasted the face of African American culture to the world, and it was one of sweetness, beauty, innocence, and pride. **OPPOSITE** The dance contest, Episode 150 on September 20, 1975.

something that should be worn proudly. It's one thing to preach a message of self-love, of "black is beautiful," during the editorial part of a show. It's another thing entirely to make good on that during the bill-paying portion of the same broadcast. Don's genius was that he was selling Afrocentricity in a bottle and we were buying it up by the ton. I still use Afro Sheen, and I think that is why I am one of the few members of my high school graduating class who doesn't have a receding hairline. It's impossible to underestimate the importance of the *Soul Train* commercials, which represented some of the first opportunities to buy television advertising and create ads targeting the African American audience. These kinds of things didn't exist before *Soul Train*, and the show's partnership with Johnson Products created openings for black writers, black actors, black directors, black producers, and black ad agencies. Even some of the dancers on the show were cast in the Johnson Products commercials. What was at work was good business sense, but also community cohesion. George E. Johnson Sr., owner of the Chicago-based Johnson Products, believed in the show's concept so much that he signed on for the long haul when *Soul Train* was still a local favorite, and Don credited this early support with the show's ability to become syndicated in the first place.

The way *Soul Train* reinvested regional word of mouth was another part of its genius. The show had taken off like a rocket when it first aired on WCIU-TV in Chicago, but Don was well

> *There were individuals at the time who were on the proverbial wish list, and before we had to wait too long, they decided to come in. Among the first were the Jackson 5. But we had to go after major people who were coming out of Chicago like the Chi-Lites and Curtis Mayfield. Jerry Butler helped me a lot in the early days to procure talent. Then Motown started to take notice and send people our way.*
>
> —Don Cornelius

aware that the only way for it to grow the way he wanted was to convince the audience and network executives that the program was the hippest trip in America. He had gotten a big act for his first episode, Gladys Knight & the Pips. That was an impressive first shot to fire, but Don needed to have artists of the same caliber in other episodes for the show to truly succeed. He called in favors from fellow Chicagoans and solicited the support of luminaries in the black music community. Charles Wright & the Watts 103rd Street Rhythm Band were on the second episode, along with Carla Thomas, and other big names followed: the Chambers Brothers, Friends of Distinction, Bobby Womack, the Dells, the Four Tops. After just one season, *Soul Train* was a runaway train.

The Flavor of *Soul Train*

We all had soul radio stations in our hometowns. Philly had some great ones. But *Soul Train* was more powerful than any local radio station. It was national, and it went deep. I know for certain that there are many songs I never heard on the radio, and would have never known existed, had it not been for the artists performing those songs on the show. Though centered on the music, the show was formatted using five unique segments:

1. **Show Opener**
2. **Headliner/Interview**
3. **Dance Segment/Soul Train Scramble Board**
4. **Support Act/Interview**
5. **The Soul Train Dance Line**

Everyone had a favorite part of the program. The *Soul Train* Dance Line became such a fan favorite that Don decided to move the segment toward the end of the show to keep viewers glued to their set for the entire running time. These segments were individually distinct, yet seamlessly fused music, style, and dance.

To write this book I combed through twenty-two years of *Soul Train* performances, from the inaugural 1971 season to Don's last season as host in 1993. I don't know which is more unfathomable—that *Soul Train* aired more than 1,100 episodes and showcased almost every genre of music imaginable, or that I could comb through the whole archive and narrow it down to three hundred of the show's most historic, hilarious, odd, sentimental, and personally influential moments. I also had to make room for my favorite special features that highlight the dancers, interviews, cameos, support acts, and off-the-cuff crazy behind-the-scenes stories of the *Soul Train* Line.

I am a Soul Snob. I'll cop to that. I was born the same year the show went national, and I watched it from the minute I could sit up on my own. Over the course of my life, I have repeatedly returned to episodes I already know by heart to interpret the dialogue, locate little grace notes and accidents, spot background events that escaped me the first time, or the fifth or the tenth. I am stunned by the dancing, astonished by the fashions, and fascinated by the commercials. I have broken codes and solved mysteries, analyzed set changes, debated over theme songs, and stolen some tricks to use in my own live performances with the Roots and as a DJ. Even in writing this book, there were moments when the light bulb went off and I jumped out of my seat. Some people learned everything they really need to know in kindergarten. Good for them. I learned everything I really need to know from *Soul Train*, long before kindergarten. I boarded the train and never got off, and that's why I continue to go to the ends of the earth to find rare footage and lost episodes. And it's not just episodes that are lost: the Scramble Board, the lighted train stage, the first *Soul Train* sign, all those things that would be worthy of a spot in the Smithsonian next to Fonzie's jacket and Archie Bunker's chair, well, they're gone. Don ordered that they be destroyed, not in a fit of pique, but because he felt that it was too expensive to store them. It saddens me a bit that he didn't preserve those artifacts. Still, it also firms my resolve to do my part to keep those things alive. You can bet your last money that I'll do my level best to make sure that *Soul Train* stays on the rails, in America's hearts and minds, and that it brings the past into the future for as long as there's a present. I hope this book brings to you what Don and *Soul Train* brought to me: love, peace, and soul.

OPPOSITE TOP The Temptations in Episode 166 on January 10, 1976.
OPPOSITE BOTTOM The Jackson 5 singing "Dancing Machine" in Episode 11 on November 3, 1973.

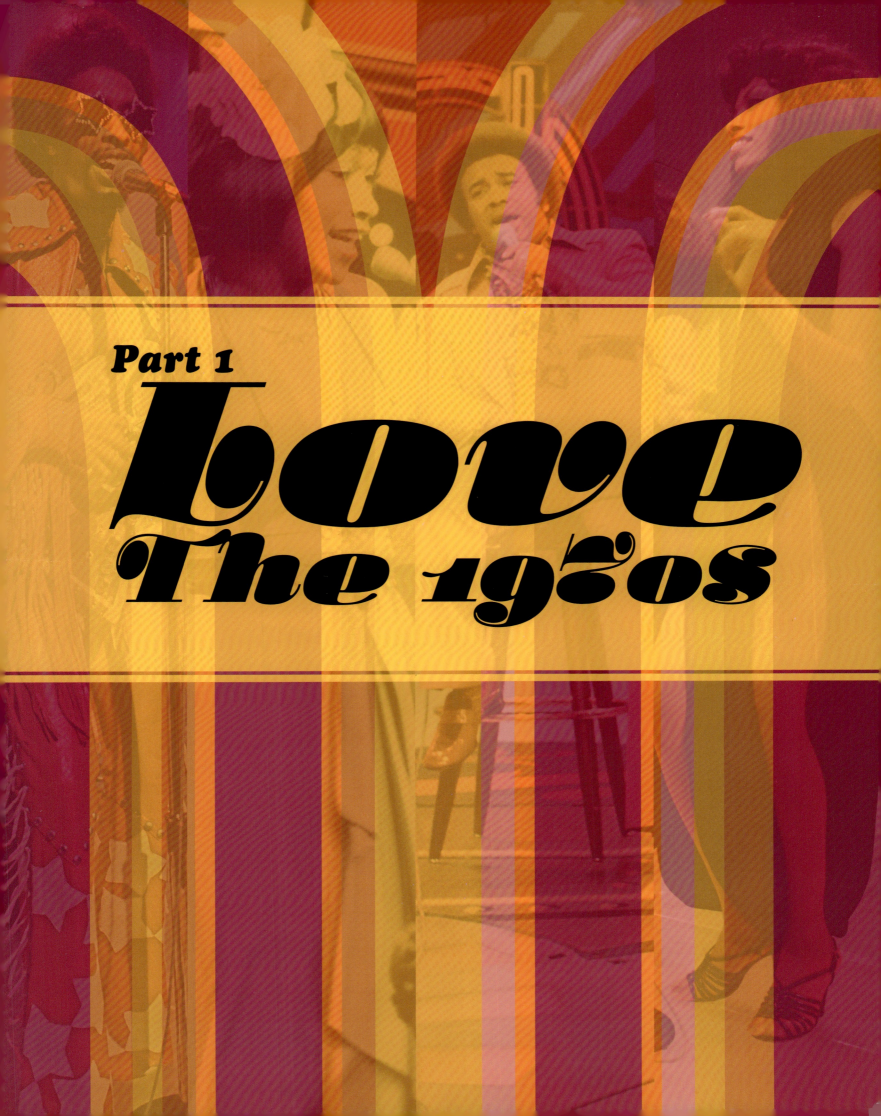

THE BIG IDEA

My *Soul Train* education began when a zigzagging animated train came barreling down the tracks, looking like it might burst right through the screen. It scared the living daylights out of me. And it wasn't just the train: I was petrified by the weird synchronized howl of Joe Cobb's "Souuuuuul Train." But the rest of it got under my skin, at once and forever: the announcer, Sid McCoy, who was one of the most famous DJs in Chicago history; Don's cool command of the camera and his ability to deliver rhyming patter in an unbroken baritone; new dances from exotic and distant places like Detroit, Atlanta, and Los Angeles; funny clothes that made girls my sister's age run for their mamas' sewing kits; and incredible artists who displayed their talents through voice, brass, strings, keys, and beat. My family turned on *Soul Train* every week expecting nothing less than a house party in our Philadelphia home. We got that and a whole lot more.

A Small Start for a Big Idea

Soul Train was born out of a local promotion Don did when he was working as a news reader and backup DJ at the Chicago radio station WVON. He and Joe Cobb, also a DJ at the station, had the idea to bring local entertainers into public high schools for shows in the auditorium, then pack up real quick and move to the next school. It felt like a train that moved around the city, so Don called it "The Soul Train." But it only worked in theory, because the cost to transport the acts would be expensive and the teens couldn't afford to buy tickets. Taking those hard-learned lessons, Don conceptualized something a little less risky—a dance program for television. The local station WCIU-TV had experimented with similar dance-oriented shows a few years earlier, so it gave Don's pitch the green light to create a daily afternoon show, which Don instinctively named *Soul Train*.

Soul Train debuted on August 17, 1970, featuring local musicians Jerry Butler, the Chi-Lites, and the Emotions. From then on, the show would always maintain a strong Chicago connection. Kids would get out of school and line up downtown at the bottom of the Chicago Board of Trade building, located in the commodities trade district. They came to dance, listen to music, and burn off some steam.

PAGE 22 Don Cornelius in Episode 207 on January 22, 1977, where he hosts Lou Rawls and L.T.D. **PAGES 24–25** A wide shot of the dancers in Episode 9 on November 27, 1971, during a performance by the Chambers Brothers, reveals how small the studio set was. **RIGHT** Roebuck "Pops" Staples, a native Chicagoan and the patriarch of the Staples Singers, in Episode 102 on June 8, 1974. **BELOW** Don's patchwork leather coat is a dead giveaway for 1971. **OPPOSITE TOP** Curtis Mayfield between takes. **OPPOSITE BOTTOM** Patrice Rushen works the Dance Line in 1971.

LEFT The Chi-Lites in Episode 173 on February 28, 1976, were the second act on the marquee. **ABOVE** The Chi-Lites headline in Episode 113 on October 19, 1974.

I thought it was the perfect name, and I always knew from day one that the show would go from city to city, just like a train. That was the whole idea.

—Don Cornelius

The first set had a local look—small and no frills. The program was shot in black and white and wasn't edited much. Part of the reason for the lack of archival footage from these early days is that the shows were never taped (though I still dream of finding footage if I look hard enough).

Don quickly learned his way around the studio, took notes on what the kids responded to, and watched what elicited positive reactions from the station execs. Everything Don picked up he used to his advantage. He made the five-day-a-week live show larger than life and popular enough to garner the support needed to syndicate.

Less than a year later, *Soul Train* got the attention of the Johnson Products Company, and on October 2, 1971, fourteen months after the first local airing of *Soul Train*, Don and his show were broadcast in seven other cities—Philadelphia, Atlanta, Detroit, Cleveland, Houston, San Francisco, and Los Angeles. Contrary to popular belief, developing *Soul Train* was

THE BIG IDEA | 29

TOP Fun was had behind the scenes in the control booth. ABOVE On November 25, 1978, Cheech & Chong made a guest appearance in Episode 277. OPPOSITE Mavis Staples in Episode 102 on June 8, 1974.

30 | SOUL TRAIN

ABOVE Episode 193 on October 16, 1976 was the Ritchie Family's turn to wow the audience with their own brand of choreographed performance. **RIGHT** Outside the Studio 4 doors, famous for crowded lines of hopeful fans. **OPPOSITE TOP** In the thick of some backstage fun, Don calls down to the control room from the studio phone. **OPPOSITE BOTTOM** The publishers of *Soul* magazine, Ken and Regina Jones, on set with Don in 1974.

not an uphill battle. It was an idea that was ripe for the times, and the show got the serious backing needed to go national. Don was one of the first African Americans to put his name on a show as "executive producer" and "creator."

When they decided to grow the show into something more sophisticated, Don and his team realized that the kind of production talent and experience they needed didn't exist in Chicago. It was coming out of the woodwork in Los Angeles. If Don wanted to do *Soul Train* in a bigger way, he had to go to LA, where a large population of the music talent he was looking for resided. The kids who would line up to dance on the show would also have a little something extra—a cutting-edge style and infectious breed of enthusiasm that could mix the pot and make it boil over. *Soul Train*'s next step was obvious, and it would be a giant leap.

Leavin' on a Morning Train to California

The first episode of the syndicated *Soul Train* boasted one of the finest and biggest acts of the day: Gladys Knight & the Pips performing the apropos "Friendship Train." Eddie Kendricks, formerly of the Temptations and recently turned solo, also performed on the first episode, as did the LA-based all-female singing group Honey Cone. Honey Cone was the show's first live vocal performance. Live performances were few and far between in the show's forty-five-year run, as lip-syncing was the standard and cost-efficient practice. As early as Episode 2, however, Charles Wright & the Watts 103rd Street Rhythm Band made the record books by being the first live band performance.

Since I am keeping score of true breakthroughs, Episode 5 on October 30, 1971, would be my pick for the first supershow—Bill Withers and Al Green, two soon-to-be powerhouses at the beginning of their careers. In hindsight, this was an iconic music moment that also represented the zeitgeist.

Bill Withers's rendition of "Harlem" was remarkable. As his vocal chords melded with the chords of his acoustic guitar, the cadence of his tapping foot led the dancers to move freely and spontaneously as they found their inner primal expression. You could just tell that the Kids had witnessed soul being set free from beneath one man's tapping right foot. And it wasn't just them, but all the young African American kids like me who were watching. Self-expression had found an outlet, and it looked ritualistic and communal as Bill sat on the small stage while dancers circled around him. It was tribal. Anyone who had the power to move people the way he could with just the bare-bones gift of his musical genius was idol worthy. I inducted Bill Withers as my childhood hero. I imagine I was not the only one.

In the second act, we met newcomer Al Green in all his statement-making glory, wearing leather

OPPOSITE Don in his dressing room prepping for a long day of taping.
BELOW AND RIGHT It was the show's 100th episode, but milestones such as this often weren't celebrated back in 1974. It is fitting, however, that returning to the show for Episode 100 on May 25, 1974, was Bill Withers, the same man who wowed me in Episode 5.

EPISODE 100, SUPERSHOW EPISODE 5 IS FAMOUS FOR BEING USED BY THE HUGHES BROTHERS IN THEIR FILM *DEAD PRESIDENTS*.

OPPOSITE TOP NFL defensive back turned actor, Fred Williamson, makes a special guest appearance in Episode 31 on September 9, 1972. **OPPOSITE BOTTOM** The Trammps in Episode 274 on November 4, 1978. **LEFT** Lyn Collins meets Don in Episode 70 on September 8, 1973. **BOTTOM** The low-tech prop responsible for the opening tunnel sequence, through which a camera carried viewers to the *Soul Train* dance floor.

hot pants, knee-high riding boots, a hot pink muscle shirt, and an oversized velvet pimp hat that made him look like the Mad Hatter on Forty-Second Street. His performance couldn't have been more opposite of Bill's—one understated and calm; the other shocking and larger than life. I mean, the guy was dancing and lip-syncing to "I'm So Tired of Being Alone," while flashing a gold chain and a murse!

In its entirety, this episode epitomized the promise of the show: an inspirational display of passion and pride by individuals gifted with limitless talent and ingenuity.

ABOVE As with every performance he gave, Al Green in Episode 135 on April 5, 1975, was a roller coaster of feverish emotions. **OPPOSITE** The many shades of Green evolved throughout the history of *Soul Train*, from Episode 93 on April 6, 1974 to Episode 347 on January 10, 1981.

Al Green

Al Green would fulfill his part of this promise by appearing on the show ten times over fourteen seasons. By his third appearance in Season 2, he would begin churning out his inspired fire and brimstone performances. On Episode 52 on March 3, 1973, he performed live with a band for the first time. Al already had a string of hits, including eight consecutive platinum and gold singles, and Don was left no choice other than to call him "Soul Music's Messiah," which is pretty much spot-on. In Episode 93 on April 6, 1974, his fourth appearance on the show, Al's performance of "Jesus Is Waiting" was his coup de grâce. He didn't even allow his broken arm to detract from his passion.

In Season 4, Episode 135 on April 5, 1975, Al appeared on *Soul Train* six months after his girlfriend committed suicide. He had the entire show to himself. I had never seen a person to whom every last syllable of his songs was sung as if his life depended on it. He began "Sha-la-la (Makes Me Happy)" and "Take Me to the River" clean, but by the second minute, his hair was messy, his tie was disheveled, and he was sweating.

It was a gift and a privilege to watch someone in his prime truly demonstrating what soul music is about. It isn't the idea of being funky or dressing hip. It's when you take all the visceral urges in you and release your inhibitions, almost automatically, as if you are possessed. Although he wouldn't become a full-fledged pastor until 1978, the way he was singing after such devastation clearly foreshadowed finding his way to the Lord.

> *Already on a string of hits, having eight consecutive platinum and gold singles, Don was left no choice other than to call Al Green 'Soul Music's Messiah.'*

That's what this episode looked like: the divine possession of Al Green. Something was on his mind, and this time there was a fire inside. By the end of his first song, he looked as if the demons of his tragedy had just been exorcised by soul.

In between possessions, Al cooled it down with "L-O-V-E," from his *Al Green Is Love* album. On a scale of one to ten, I give it an eleven. Even his drummer was inspired and did an unorthodox drum solo with his teeth. I tried to do it, and it hurts. I wouldn't recommend it to anyone who loves their teeth.

SHADES OF GREEN

The First Family of Soul (Train)

If Episode 5 was the promise of *Soul Train*, then the Jackson 5 was the promise of the civil rights era, Martin Luther King Jr.'s vision of a generation not having to bleed for human rights. Manifested in five brothers from Gary, Indiana, was the *new* American promise. They also represented Don's dream come to fruition, an act that could be the pride of the African American community yet loved by all. Their big Afro hair was the look of the Black Panthers, their clothes were Bay Area hippie, their vocals were Detroit Motown harmony, and their appeal and dancing were off the charts, beyond racial lines—international.

Don knew that it was their performances that ultimately gave the show the credibility to stay on the air and really connect with youth. Episode 35 on October 7, 1972, marked the first appearance by the Jackson 5 family on *Soul Train*, and it was key in luring kids my age (I was three at the time) and keeping them glued to *Soul Train* for years to come. The new generation would no longer perceive *Soul Train* as an adult's show with yesteryear performers doing the Bump.

I'm trying to use euphemisms here, trying to avoid saying there was no television for black folks.

The Ubiquitous Jacksons

The Jackson brothers appeared on *Soul Train* four times over eight years. The legacy of the original brotherhood would span all four decades of the show. The Jackson family became synonymous with *Soul Train*—from Michael Jackson's famed solo performance to promote the "Dancing Machine" album during Episode 111 on October 5, 1974, to Jermaine Jackson breaking out acts of his own and Randy's and Marlon's solo performances in 1978 and 1987, respectively, to sisters La Toya and Rebbie vying for the spotlight, to the singing debut of the sweet and sensational Janet, who became a force all her own, in Episode 408 on December 18, 1982.

THE BIG IDEA | **41**

PAGES 40-41 In Episode 77 on November 3, 1973, the Jackson 5 had the stage all to themselves, performing songs: "Dancing Machine," "Don't Say Goodbye Again," "Get It Together," and two solo spots, one for Jermaine, "You're in Good Hands," and one for Michael, "With a Child's Heart." PAGES 42-43 As a young boy, it was hard not to wish to be just like the Jacksons. ABOVE The Jackson 5 in Episode 77 helped reinforce my decision never to get rid of my Afro. BELOW *Soul Train* was the place where many kids were introduced to lesser-known instruments. In Episode 35 on October 7, 1972, Randy on the bongos gave viewers a treat. RIGHT As I got older, it was hard not to wish to be near little sister Janet. Here she is in Episode 342 on November 8, 1980, during which Don introduced older sister La Toya. OPPOSITE Michael Jackson during his solo show, Episode 111 on October 5, 1974.

SOUL TRAIN

OPPOSITE Michael Jackson singing in Episode 168 on January 24, 1976. ABOVE Randy Jackson is interviewed by Don in Episode 77. RIGHT The Jacksons' father and manager, Joe Jackson, behind the scenes with Don and Dick Griffey during Episode 111.

THE ACTS

The early 1970s were a shaky time for black music. The civil rights era had seen giant steps forward in jazz, soul, and black pop; as the '70s dawned, there was a pause and uncertainty regarding the next step. Would Motown, which had played such an important and historical role in the racial integration of soul music, be as successful in the new decade? What about Stax or Hi, or Atlantic for that matter? Would the artists who had evolved over the course of America's most tumultuous decade be able to move forward again? No matter who you were, what label backed you, or how successful you had been, no matter if you were Aretha Franklin or Marvin Gaye or Stevie Wonder, those first years of the '70s required you to go through a creative tollbooth, to slow to a stop and start all over again.

PAGE 48 On May 10, 1975, Dionne Warwick headlined Episode 140. **TOP** The 5th Dimension in Episode 115 on November 2, 1974. **ABOVE** Smokey Robinson in Episode 144 on June 14, 1975. **RIGHT** Barry White mingles with the audience in Episode 76 on October 27, 1973.

James Brown, for one, decided to fire his entire band and start over with younger musicians. Many of the Delta blues musicians were getting discovered by the new regime of rock royalty crowned by the British invasion and had to contextualize their music to appeal to fans of the Beatles, the Rolling Stones, and Cream. Additionally, artists shifted music genres, relationships severed, new alliances formed, and an audience with more sophisticated and eclectic musical tastes emerged. With so much going on, 1971 to 1973 was a crucial period for black music. Those who showed the way had died. Jimi Hendrix had to leave this world in order for acts like the Isley Brothers, Parliament, Funkadelic, Sly & the Family Stone, and Rick James to find the creative license to take black music where *they* wanted it to go, transforming soul music to *funk*.

THE ACTS | 51

OPPOSITE TOP The Dynamic Superiors in Episode 120 on December 21, 1974. **OPPOSITE BOTTOM** Rolling a piano out on the *Soul Train* stage meant an awe-inspiring performance every time; case in point, Ashford & Simpson's appearance on December 8, 1973, in Episode 82. **LEFT** The Isley Brothers in Episode 32 on September 16, 1972. **BELOW** Natalie Cole in Episode 214 on March 12, 1977.

Stevie Wonder

But funk wasn't the only new music expression born in the '70s. In black music, revolutionary ideas take about the first three years of a new decade to hold. And *Soul Train* benefited greatly from being in the right place at the right time. By 1973, there was a new establishment, and many a *Soul Train* episode revealed it. In **EPISODE 46 ON JANUARY 13, 1973**, Stevie Wonder debuted "Superstition." It was easily one of the top ten episodes of all time. He invited God into his brain and then channeled divinity through his fingers, becoming the conduit for the greatest music celebrated since the Beatles.

Stevie's performance was extraordinary, but what left the audience truly breathless was when he told Don that he'd written an impromptu theme song in his head. With the dancers gathered around the piano, as if ready to be dipped in a pool of holy water, Stevie's fingers began to roll, and he directed the *Soul Train* Dancers to "give me some assistance," "put your hands together," "clap soft." He sang the instant composition "*Soul Train* with Don Cornelius." Infectious and funny, he sang the lyrics as if he were at a revival meeting. And the crowd sang repeatedly in unison to Stevie's directive: "Where all the brothers and sisters get together!"

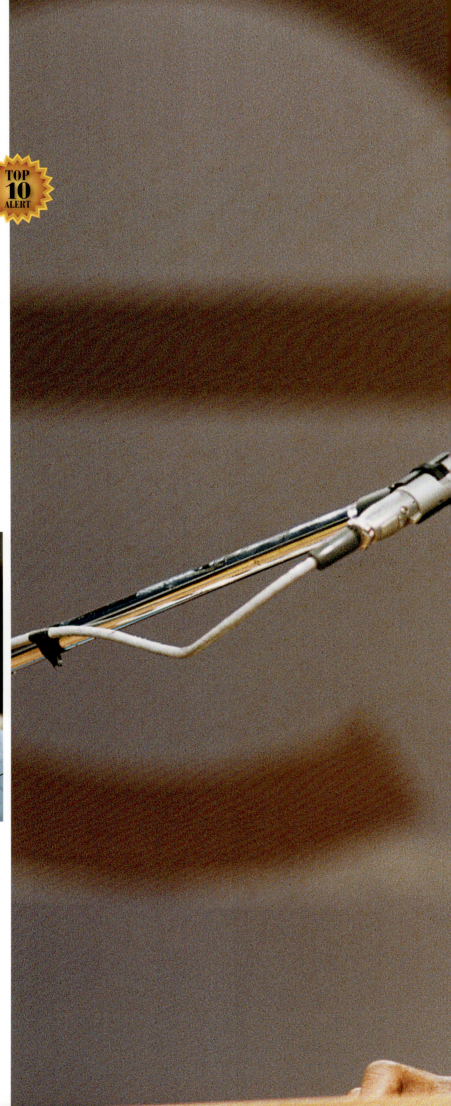

PAGES 54-55 Sly & the Family Stone in Episode 105 on June 29, 1974. **ABOVE** One of my "top tens" for all-time favorite, Episode 46 boasted a great interview and performances. Every time I watch Stevie Wonder during this episode, I want to thank him. **RIGHT** Stevie performing "Superstition."

Marvin Gaye

The effect of 1973 was pivotal for *Soul Train*, as that year also marked the second of Marvin Gaye's one-two punch for self-producing. His first punch was his political magnum opus "What's Going On?" It was followed by his sexual magnum opus "Let's Get It On."

Marvin had been an unnecessarily reluctant performer since 1968, after his most successful duet partner, Tammi Terrell ("Ain't Nothing Like the Real Thing" and "Ain't No Mountain High Enough," among others), collapsed in his arms on stage. Her death traumatized and disillusioned Marvin, compelling him to take a sabbatical from performing publicly and recording on a regular basis. Tired of being the prince and puppet of Motown, Marvin vowed to rebel and grew his beard long and pursued a football career with the Detroit Lions. Berry Gordy called the owner of the Lions and tried to dissuade him from allowing Marvin on the team. Nevertheless, Marvin continued to work out with the Lions.

Meanwhile, Marvin's brother, Frankie, had come home from Vietnam, inspiring Marvin toward a more political approach to his music, thus giving birth to "What's Going On?" Motown hated it, but Marvin insisted, "This is what you're getting." The bar talk and background voices in the recording are the voices of the Detroit Lions team. Insecure and rusty, Marvin wouldn't go on stage to perform the song, except for one time in Washington, DC.

By 1973, if Marvin's career was to survive, he needed to establish himself with a new generation who had not seen him perform in six years. With "Let's Get It On" in his back pocket, he came out of the shadows to return to the public eye on *Soul Train*, in Episode 89 on February 16, 1974.

BELOW Marvin managed to transcend the limitations of lip-syncing in Episode 89.

ABOVE Fraternizing with the Kids for a fiery performance, Marvin ignites the floor in Episode 89. **LEFT** On May 7, 1977, Marvin has Episode 222 all to himself.

Soft-spoken and humble, Marvin spoke to the audience, offering them accolades, as if it were his own concert. Don rarely allowed artists the privilege of addressing the audience without his supervision. Only Bill Withers, Gladys Knight, Chuck Berry, and Sly Stone shared the honor.

I had never seen a performance in which the dancers were permitted to surround the stage like a ring. But there they were, with Marvin in the center. His deep insecurity was unfounded: once he was on that stage, the audience was putty in his hands. Seeing that was enough for me to dismiss whatever fears and insecurities he had about himself, because every grieving soul in that audience hung on his every word.

THE ACTS | 59

OPPOSITE Chuck Berry is the main event in Episode 66 on July 7, 1973. **ABOVE** Chuck takes a break with the crew in Episode 66.

Rock Royalty Sink or Swim

The pressure of a new era did not discriminate, and many of the acts of previous decades stepped up their game in order to stay in it. Episode 16 on January 15, 1972, marked the beginning of true judgment day. Booking Little Richard seemed a strategic move on Don's part—attempting to attract audiences on both sides of the generational Mason-Dixon line—but Little Richard didn't exactly translate to the younger kids coming of age in the '70s. Even though he was actively recording in the '70s, his invitation to the show felt more like an homage to the birth of rock and roll. Don even acknowledged Little Richard as the "King of Rock 'n' Roll," which was an important indicator of *Soul Train*'s role as a history teacher, especially for younger generations who didn't understand how one could take gospel music, add a salacious rhythm, and make kids dance all over America.

Don also booked many others from days gone by, such as Rufus Thomas, who, by 1973, was one of the oldest working performers. He started in the business in the '40s, but thanks to *Soul Train* would go on to deliver some of his most significant hits during the early '70s. His music inspired *Soul Train* dance trends like the Funky Chicken, the Breakdown, the Push and Pull, and the Funky Penguin. Other rock royalty trying to cross the bridge to modern times included Jackie Wilson, who in Episode 22 on February 26, 1972, had the chance to perform his massive hit "Your Love Keeps Lifting Me Higher." Had it not been for Jackie's coma a year after this appearance and his untimely death in 1984, *Soul Train* might have helped him rival James Brown, who revived his own career several times over the decades.

THE ACTS

ABOVE The Bar-Kays were interviewed by Don in Episode 31 on September 9, 1972. **OPPOSITE** Johnny Mathis's interview with Don in Episode 88 on February 9, 1974.

JOHNNY MATHIS

Johnny Mathis was in an especially precarious position because the artists of the 1950s who were trying to transfer to the '70s came from soul or doo-wop. This established '50s crooner known for his pop vocals was not only dealing with staying relevant but was contending with finding a more urban sound. It was a double strike against the veteran who was only in his thirties. But he succeeded by becoming the greatest ballad singer of all time with hits like "Foolish," which he performed on Episode 88, on February 9, 1974, when Don introduced him as "the gifted Johnny Mathis." Any artist who survived after changing his genre more than twenty years after he began his career was extremely lucky.

Motown and *Soul Train*

When Martha and the Vandellas appeared on *Soul Train* in Episode 7 on November 13, 1971, they solidified the relationship between the show and Motown. *Soul Train* helped Motown leave the '60s behind and find its way in the '70s, and Motown sent great bookings Don's way. Not only had Motown originated legends like the Marvelettes, the Four Tops, Diana Ross and the Supremes, Stevie Wonder, the Jackson 5, Marvin Gaye, and the Spinners, but in doing so Motown also helped heal the wounds left behind by the civil rights era. The music appealed to blacks and whites—kids of all colors who wanted to learn about each other. Through the music, they could meet at a crossroads.

By 1972, Motown was feeling the need to leave its local grassroots foundation and completed its expansion into motion pictures in LA, which just so happened to coincide with *Soul Train*'s relocation from Chicago to LA. The move meant making sacrifices, especially for Motown, which had to leave the session band and some local celebrity artists behind. Motown gained a certain amount of class upon arriving in LA, and it needed a way to christen its new image as a powerhouse. *Soul Train* was it. From then on, *Soul Train* and Motown were on a road to making beautiful music together for the next twenty years.

RIGHT A Ross-less Supremes in Episode 146 on August 23, 1975.
BELOW The Temptations in Episode 416 on June 4, 1983 represented the styles of the '70s well into the '80s.

LEFT The Four Tops in Episode 196 on November 6, 1976.

THE ACTS 65

SOUL TRAIN

OPPOSITE TOP Richard Pryor is a gas of a guest host in Episode 145 on June 21, 1975. **OPPOSITE BOTTOM** The Spinners in Episode 191 on October 2, 1976. **TOP** Billy Preston with Ronnie Wood in Episode 208 on January 29, 1977. **ABOVE** The Temptations.

THE ACTS

Jazzin' Up *Soul Train*

The first ten years of *Soul Train* exemplified Don's open-mindedness regarding musical genres. Artists who didn't fit the "soul mold" were respected and welcomed with open arms. Inviting several jazz musicians to the show was a continuation on the theme of educating young people about music and musical history. Notable acts included South African trumpeter Hugh Masekela, who, as one of the few international guests, spoke about how his music protested apartheid, slavery, and his country's government.

ABOVE Hugh Masekela sounds off a political message as well as a musical one in Episode 101 on June 1, 1974. **LEFT** Another of Don's Chicagoans, Ramsey Lewis, in Episode 104 on June 22, 1974. **OPPOSITE TOP** Herbie Hancock puts his signature on the show in Episode 110 on September 28, 1974. **OPPOSITE BOTTOM** Ramsey Lewis brings jazz to *Soul Train*.

THE ACTS

Appealing to a New Generation

Soul Train had hit its stride by 1973. The popularity of the show had expanded so that it became impossible for anyone to ignore *Soul Train*'s power and influence, especially among young people. In many ways Don believed that the reason he started getting the bigger bookings like James Brown and Aretha Franklin was because some young person in their lives insisted they were missing the hippest trip in America, and therefore the biggest chance to stay relevant to the next generation.

IKE & TINA TURNER

A new day arrived for *Soul Train* when Ike & Tina Turner performed in Episode 30 on April 22, 1972. Until then, *Soul Train* had not been able to attract a nontraditional soul superact. Because Ike & Tina Turner were an international sensation in the same vein as the Beatles and the Stones, their appearance on the show established *Soul Train*'s credibility. I mean, when

BELOW The Kids grooved to Ike & Tina Turner in Episode 124 on January 18, 1975. **BOTTOM** Tina is a force to reckon with in Episode 124. **RIGHT** Ike & Tina Turner in Episode 30 on April 22, 1972.

OPPOSITE Aretha Franklin in Episode 197 on November 13, 1976.
ABOVE Aretha Franklin in Episode 56 on April 14, 1973. **RIGHT** Just like the Jacksons, the Sylvers grew up on *Soul Train*.

A FAMILY AFFAIR
THE SYLVERS AND THE FIVE STAIRSTEPS

Episode 39 on November 4, 1972, hosted the Sylvers, the only act that, I believe, could rival the Jackson 5 in terms of talent (and possibly the tallest pyramid of empty bottles of Ultra Sheen). When the act began, it had seven brothers and sisters. Two more would join by 1975. They were on the show six times and produced some significant hits like "Boogie Fever," but never achieved the status of the Jacksons. The same went for the Five Stairsteps, who appeared on Episode 9, November 27, 1971, and couldn't have been a cuter family group, but they came too early to enjoy the payoff of being America's most loved boy band.

My theory on why these two family bands were overshadowed by the Jackson 5, particularly by Michael Jackson, is rooted in the year the members were born. Michael was born in 1958, which made him thirteen during *Soul Train*'s first season. If he had been under thirteen, he would have been too young to be taken seriously. If Michael had been over thirteen, it would have been a case of "hide your daughters." The Sylvers and the Five Stairsteps were the right idea, but came just a tad too soon. Timing is everything—although it doesn't hurt having the Motown machine behind you either.

Mick Jagger was going around telling everyone he was the male version of Tina Turner, and then Tina Turner showed up in LA to perform to a bunch of dancing teenagers, *Soul Train* was destined to enter a new phase. The floodgates opened.

ARETHA FRANKLIN

When Aretha Franklin showed up in Episode 56 on April 14, 1973, she told Don in her interview, "My kids love the show, and I want to be a part of it." She then went on to acknowledge the power of the show, singing "Rock Steady." It took two and a half years for the show to penetrate the kids' consciousness, and now the parents wanted their piece of the pie.

THE ACTS

ABOVE Fred Wesley & The J.B.'s in Episode 108 on September 14, 1974. **OPPOSITE** James Brown on the same episode as his protégés, Fred Wesley & The J.B.'s, Lyn Collins, and Sweet Charles.

Tribute to James Brown

For every year that went by, James Brown had to prove all over again that he was worthy of his title "Godfather of Soul." For Episode 49 on February 10, 1973, just shy of forty, James was given the first "salute to" show—an entire hour devoted to his performances. Don replaced the signature *Soul Train* backdrop with a customized one that read "James is #1," written in the same font *Soul Train* used for its own name.

The "Salute to James Brown" episode was crucial for the singer and one of my personal favorites, but not because he performed "Super Bad." It's a *Soul Train* geek reason and possibly a band leader thing. This period marked James's third band incarnation. His previous band had been the New Breed, which included then eighteen-year-old Bootsy Collins on bass. Brown was known to lose or fire band members in the blink of an eye, and he started all over again in this episode to prove that he'd be as important in '73 as he had been in the '50s and '60s. James also was known to fine musicians for so much as having a wrinkled jacket, so I can only imagine how stressful it was being in a band in which you had to play your instrument to perfection while keeping your eye on James to avoid missing any type of cue. I saw second drummer Melvin Parker do just that, except he gave James a cold stare. But James was and still is one of the tightest band leaders of his generation. As a band leader myself, I appreciate watching this discipline.

Episode 108 on September 14, 1974, was the second James Brown tribute show, "James Brown & the First Family of Soul," and I treasure every moment of it to this day. Even in a world consisting of constant highs, there were a few episodes that were able to go far beyond the heavens, and one that I have in mind tells the story of a man who knew he was a superhero and a world that was in need of one. He arrived on this show with a thirteen-piece band and protégés Lyn Collins and Sweet Charles, and he performed on a custom-built platform compliments of Don so that James's eight-year-old daughter, Deanna, could dance next to her dad. James even arranged for nineteen-year-old Al Sharpton to present him with "the black record award," an unofficial award for his hit song "Payback," solidifying the song as the black anthem of the time. James made five costume changes in this one show, the most for any performer in the show's entire run.

> *James Brown was and still is one of the tightest band leaders of his generation.*

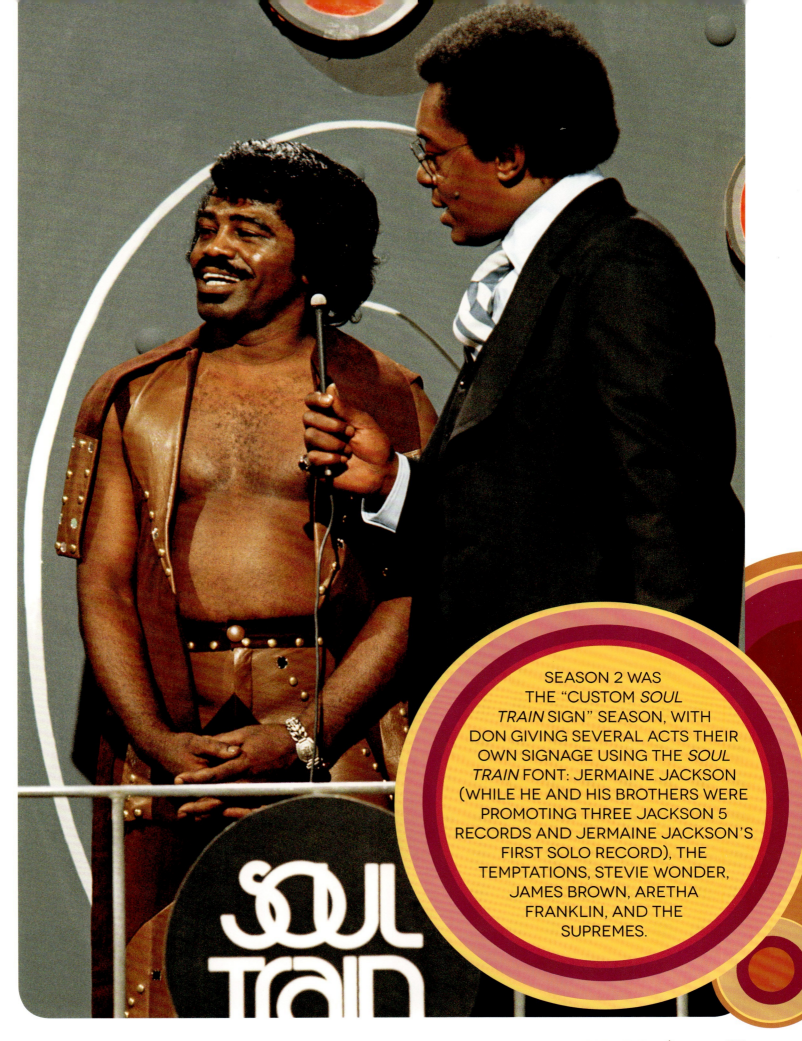

SEASON 2 WAS THE "CUSTOM *SOUL TRAIN* SIGN" SEASON, WITH DON GIVING SEVERAL ACTS THEIR OWN SIGNAGE USING THE *SOUL TRAIN* FONT: JERMAINE JACKSON (WHILE HE AND HIS BROTHERS WERE PROMOTING THREE JACKSON 5 RECORDS AND JERMAINE JACKSON'S FIRST SOLO RECORD), THE TEMPTATIONS, STEVIE WONDER, JAMES BROWN, ARETHA FRANKLIN, AND THE SUPREMES.

THE ACTS

Funk Fever

As soul musicians blended more of an electric rhythmic beat into their music, funk became the new breed of black music, and had the state of Ohio to thank for it. In the early '70s, there was a funk revolution in the Midwest, and Ohio secretly became the funk capital of the United States, with the Ohio Players and its eight members being the flagship artists of the revolution. James Brown recognized this early. He established his entire operation in Cincinnati and began producing records turning out this type of music, which influenced local bands. *Soul Train* helped funk come out of its musical closet by giving airtime to more elusive acts like Mandrill, Tower of Power, Rufus featuring Chaka Khan, B.T. Express, the Kay-Gees, Bootsy's Rubber Band, Average White Band, Graham Central Station, the Brothers Johnson, and Chuck Brown and the Soul Searchers, the father of go-go music, a subgenre of funk.

Episode 69's nod to funk group Mandrill stands out for me, because I have "borrowed" their presentation for use in the Roots' live performances. Mandrill didn't have a lead singer. Everyone sang together in a Greek chorus style. I describe them as an urban version of Santana, fusing soul and rock and mixing it with Latin rhythm. The episode aired on September 1, 1973, and in it Mandrill made an unorthodox, albeit effective, entrance to the stage, marching through the audience in a processional of percussion, banging cowbells and shaking tambourines. It was electric. Roots fans will note that I use the same trick because of the communal effect Mandrill had on this episode's *Soul Train* audience.

OPPOSITE TOP The Ohio Players in Episode 116 on November 9, 1974. **OPPOSITE BOTTOM** Bootsy's Rubber Band in Episode 212 on February 26, 1977. **TOP** Tower of Power in Episode 126 on February 1, 1975. **ABOVE** In Episode 141 on May 17, 1975, Claude "Coffee" Cave II, on keyboards, fit right in with his fellow showmen of Mandrill, who never failed to execute the funk in sound and in style.

THE ACTS | 77

The Supergroup Sensation

If funk music wasn't blowing everybody's minds, the number of band members in many of the groups of the decade was mind-boggling. These supergroup sensations became the norm of the '70s and were also a supersized challenge to appear on the *Soul Train* set. If you didn't see it, you wouldn't have believed that somehow Barry White's sixty-six-member Love Unlimited Orchestra squeezed onto the set in Episode 142 on May 24, 1975. When KC & the Sunshine Band showed up on Episode 199 on November 27, 1976, they stuffed their eleven members on the stage. Earth, Wind & Fire didn't bother trying getting their entire horn section on the set for Episode 267 on September 16, 1978, so instead they aired footage from one of their concerts.

ABOVE Buddy Miles in Episode 130 on March 1, 1975. **TOP** Brass Construction in Episode 323 on March 29, 1980. **MIDDLE** War in Episode 317 on February 2, 1980. **RIGHT** In case you can't read the sign, this is a shot of Barry White and Love Unlimited Orchestra in Episode 142 on May 24, 1975.

THE ACTS | 79

LEFT The Pointer Sisters in Episode 79 on November 17, 1973 were still in their '40s jazzy overtones before their '80s pop makeover. **TOP** L.T.D. in Episode 248 on February 4, 1978. **ABOVE** Originating with L.T.D., Jeffrey Osborne didn't do too poorly for himself in the crossover transition of the '80s.

Cash Chameleons

Many bands born in the '60s were able to survive and thrive in a new decade that brought fast and furious changes to black music, beginning with the emergence of funk. Some bands not only reinvented their sound, changed their genres altogether (sometimes several times), and stayed relevant, but they also existed long enough to see through to the '80s and achieve absolute pay dirt.

THE POINTER SISTERS

The Pointer Sisters were not an overnight success. They started out as a black answer to the Andrews Sisters' music—a '40s-centric jazz singing style infused with bebop. When I first saw the Pointer Sisters on Episode 79 on November 17, 1973, they ambitiously sang live to a track of the late-1950s jazz masterpiece "Cloudburst" by Lambert, Hendricks & Ross. The up-tempo and intricate composition of 170 beats per minute made this

THE ACTS

an extremely challenging song, requiring vocals at a breakneck speed. The song was so rapid that the dancers didn't dance, but watched in amazement as they tried to decipher the lyrics, which were delivered as if an auctioneer were lighting up the stage at Birdland. And because they weren't singing with a live band, but to a jazz track of the instrumental, their timing had to be air-tight. As a vocal quartet, the four sisters performed the song's stops and starts on a dime, as if walking a tightrope a hundred feet from the ground with their eyes closed.

The Pointer Sisters did a lot of vocal acrobatics in their subsequent performances, but come 1975, they ditched their Chattanooga kitschy act and went straight to funky. They, too, would be able to keep up with the onslaught of music genres and achieve the crossover dream in the '80s.

THE COMMODORES

The Commodores were a funk band that happened to let the sax player sing lead on a few songs and found themselves turning from funk to the earliest inclination of "churban" (adult contemporary urban music). The authors of "Brick House," "Machine Gun," and "I Feel Sanctified" were also able to do in a snap "Three Times a Lady," "Still," and "Sail On." In their effort to jump the funk ship, Lionel Richie did one better and went solo.

Don gave the Commodores a tribute show in Episode 315, December 8, 1979, in which an in-depth interview revealed things I never knew about them. For starters, their quest from Tuskegee, Alabama, to Harlem, New York, in search of a manager, whom they found in Benny Ashburn. I was inspired by their leap-of-faith story that led to their ultimate success, but not without first having their van and valuable equipment stolen within an hour of hitting the road. Their performance of "Still" turned out to be so powerful that it caused one dancer to break down in a pool of tears.

TOP LEFT June Pointer in Episode 79 on November 17, 1973. **TOP RIGHT** In Episode 121 on December 28, 1974, Lionel Richie was lead singer of the Commodores. **ABOVE** In Episode 152 on October 4, 1975, the Pointer Sisters are back with a more subdued look, but there's still a long way to go to hit pay dirt.

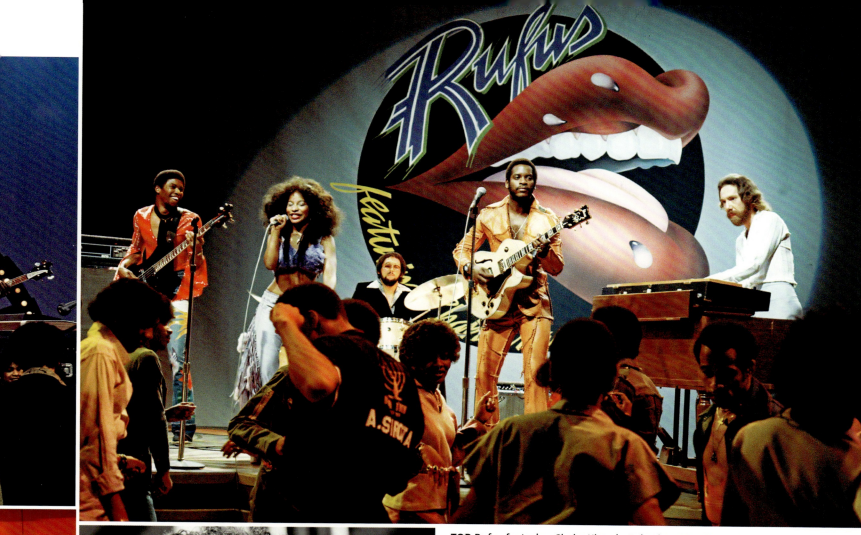

TOP Rufus featuring Chaka Khan in Episode 162 on December 13, 1975.
LEFT Chaka Khan.

RUFUS

Because *Soul Train* provided many acts with their inaugural televised performance, many a band would come off as shy or amateurish, and Rufus did not appear to be a well-oiled machine—at first. But with each Rufus appearance, audiences witnessed the band's growth and increasing sophistication in style and confidence. The most notable change was in the slow and steady emergence of Chaka Khan, who went from reserved and shy to a brilliant, fiery, wild child vocalist by the mid-'70s period of *Soul Train*. In their first appearance in Episode 73 on September 29, 1973, Chaka hid beneath an oversized denim applejack hat, performing 1973's "Whoever's Thrilling You (Is Killing Me)." By three years later, she had fully blossomed into her signature sultriness when she stunned viewers with "Dance Wit Me," in Episode 183. "Dance Wit Me" was such a massive hit that Rufus and Chaka returned for a rare encore performance twenty-six episodes later.

THE ACTS

KOOL & THE GANG

Kool & the Gang began as a jazz group in the 1960s. Invited on the show in Season 1 as the third act on Episode 22, which aired on February 26, 1972, the group demonstrated their "kool jazz." They changed their genre in Season 3 and were promoted to second act on **EPISODE 86 ON JANUARY 12, 1974**, performing their very funky song "Funky Stuff" (released as a single in 1973). But while this performance enthralled Don and the dancers, it was usurped by their second performance on the same episode, with the song "Jungle Boogie."

"Jungle Boogie" was the B-side of the *Funky Stuff* album. The eight-piece band boasted some major brass, and the supergroup shook up the house. The raw beat led the room of

SONGS TWICE AS NICE

In addition to Kool & the Gang, these acts also double-dipped: Joe Tex ("I Gotcha"), Honey Cone ("Want Ads"), Gladys Knight & the Pips ("Neither One of Us"), Rufus with Chaka Khan ("Dance Wit Me"), the Sylvers ("Boogie Fever"), DeBarge ("I Like It"), Anita Baker ("Angel"), and Smokey Robinson ("Turn Your Lights Down Low"). The longest span of time between a song being used twice goes to the O'Jays, who debuted "Used to Be My Girl" on August 1, 1978, and returned ten years later on Episode 576, October 1, 1988, with the same song in their back pocket. A song frozen in time being performed by a group that wasn't unmarked by a decade of aging was a little surreal.

LEFT Kool & the Gang make *Soul Train* history in Episode 103 on June 15, 1974. **ABOVE** In 1978, The O'Jays were at the height of success with their recently released album *So Full of Love*.

dancers unconsciously toward a maniacal dance style—down to the ground, arms flailing in the air, elbows flapping, fingers snapping, and spontaneous screams of painful pleasure as Robert Mickens's trumpet wailed over harmonious saxophones and Dennis "DT" Thomas's tenor horn. Don was so stunned by the dancers' reactions that he famously admitted to the band during the interview portion of the show that he had been so busy with his work on the show that he never bothered to check the B-side. He heard "Jungle Boogie" for the first time at the taping of the episode. The effect of the entire package—song, performance, dancers—was so powerful that Don invited Kool & the Gang back to perform the same two songs that same season. Episode 103—just five months later—marked the first time on the show that a band double-dipped both of their performances. Acts had repeated one song before, but never more.

THE ACTS

TOP LEFT Donna Summer in Episode 176 on March 20, 1976. **LEFT** Frankie Valli in Episode 275 on November 11, 1978. **ABOVE** Donna Summer returns in Episode 203 on December 25, 1976. **OPPOSITE** Gerald Brown of The *Soul Train* Gang in Episode 170 on February 7, 1976. **PAGES 88–89** Village People in Episode 328 on May 3, 1980.

Disco: A Brief Derailing? Or a Change with the Times?

When Season 3 debuted on August 25, 1973, *Soul Train*'s opening animation was more sophisticated and professional, showcasing a train leaving Chicago and traveling across a map to its final destination in Los Angeles. The train had arrived and so had the show. It also had a new theme song, "The Sound of Philadelphia (TSOP)," which Don admits he foolishly did not permit to be called "Soul Train." Don didn't think the song by Kenny Gamble and Leon Huff would be a number-one pop hit and didn't yet know the influence his show would have on pop culture. The failure to name the theme song after the show was Don's only regret regarding the show. "TSOP" turned out to be the most iconic and well-liked of the show's many theme songs (but not by me, since my vote goes to O'Bryan's "Soul Train's a Comin'" remix from 1984–1987). By 1973–1974 a new era was in full swing and imprinted itself in the music, and "TSOP" was a song that represented the sound of the new music era—disco.

It is my opinion that black music came to a screeching halt when disco arrived. Funk continued to appeal to its core fans, but would not be embraced commercially. Black music has always been defined and contextualized by gospel, and this marked the first time an era in black music placed less emphasis on gospel. Disco had nothing to do with religion—unless your religion was hedonism.

This fast, lush-sounding music with its orchestration and Latin percussion mixed with the steady syncopated pocket of the drums created a synergy never heard before in music. The charge of the *Shaft* soundtrack, in which Isaac Hayes introduced the idea of mixing orchestral strings with dance music, inspired Kenny Gamble and Leon Huff to run with the musical style, until ultimately the sound would be credited to Barry White.

Don admitted that it blindsided him. He had a choice to make: embrace disco or ignore it. The ninth episode of Season 6, aired on October 16, 1976, marked the beginning of Don's embracement of disco as he made strides to face it head-on. Gone were the iconic *Soul Train* logo and the tracks that adorned that logo, the train on the stage that was danced upon, the tunnels that the camera rolled through to the main set—all in order to present a more sophisticated disco image, which to me begs the question: "Isn't that an oxymoron?"

To me, the essence of the show's scenery was stripped away. A small disco ball with the *Soul Train* logo in its center was the new focal point. The stage was a glass rectangle with spotlights underneath, and the animation put you more in a disco frame of mind than a soul frame of mind. I would be remiss if I didn't admit that this is my least favorite of the "classic" periods of *Soul Train*. I can't deny the disco era one fact, though: it was a guilty pleasure for many. I'm not naming any names.

Still, the hits were unstoppable. That year, Donna Summer demonstrated her sounds of self-love that gave pause to every parent with her hit "Love to Love You Baby," and KC and the Sunshine Band shook their booties. *Grease* was the word with the resurgence of the evergreen Frankie Valli in Episode 275 on November 11, 1978. And who could ignore the female national anthem that Gloria Gaynor performed in Episode 292 on March 10, 1979, when the opening sweep of the piano keys in "I Will Survive" sent chills down the spine of every female dancer on the *Soul Train* set, as well as every male dancer, except in a different way.

SOUL TRAIN RECORDS

The *Soul Train* brand was unstoppable, and Don and Dick Griffey embarked on a new business venture in 1975—their own record label, Soul Train Records. The quintet group called the *Soul Train* Gang was formed and charged with singing the show's new 1975 theme song, simply titled "Soul Train '75." Other groups formed by the label included the Whispers, Shalamar (with dancers Jeffrey Daniel and Jody Watley), and Lakeside. Griffey wound up taking sole ownership of the label in 1977 and changed the name to Solar. He remained good friends with Don, often sending many of his acts to *Soul Train* for years to come. The Whispers hold the record of appearing on *Soul Train* the most times—sixteen.

THE ACTS

THE MOVES

When I was growing up, *Soul Train* was cool, and cool was *Soul Train*. This was well before the dawn of the VCR, so the only way you could ensure that you remembered everything about a *Soul Train* episode was to, well, remember everything. This was doubly true for the dancers. My cousins and I would watch them closely, as intent as any scientist in the field. "You all see that?" one of us would say, shoving the others to attention. "You all see that?" We'd look around to make sure we hadn't seen it wrong and then head to the mirror to practice. After the show, we'd go out into the street to show off our new moves, where we discovered that most everybody in the neighborhood had the same idea.

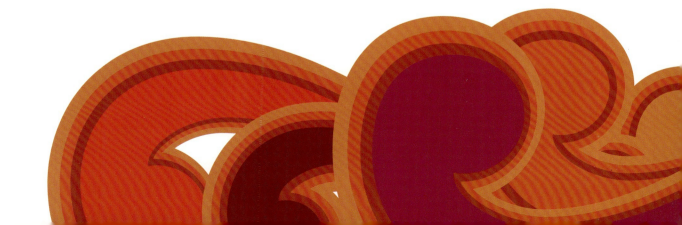

Don once stated that the *Soul Train* Dancers were always intended to be the "true stars of the show." Whether or not he was able to book the big-name musical acts, he could always count on his dancers, in all their magnetic and stylish glory, to entertain, inspire, and wow the viewers. As it turns out, the unintentional modus operandi of *Soul Train* was to feature an act on its rise or on its descent, but never while at the top of its game. So ultimately the dancers were the ones who left indelible marks on the audience.

Season 1 Dancers

From 1971 to 1975, the dancers were called the *Soul Train* Gang, but as the word *gang* took on a negative connotation, Don changed the name to the *Soul Train* Dancers. He did, however, repurpose *Soul Train* Gang for a soul music group that he and Dick Griffey formed in 1975 for Soul Train Records.

According to Don, *Soul Train* was first and foremost a dance show, so he sought out people who looked good on camera and danced well. But when Don arrived in LA and began meeting the kids who eagerly auditioned their contortions, acrobatics, and funky "street" dance styles, he realized that he got much more than he bargained for—and in a good way.

MEET THE CAST
- Charles "Robot" Washington
- Pat Davis
- Thelma Davis
- Damita Jo Freeman
- Jimmy "Scoo B Doo" Foster
- A dance troupe known and named for its pop-and-lock moves, the Lockers included Don "Campbellock" Campbell, Leo "Fluky Luke" Williamson, Adolfo "Shabba Doo" Quinones, Greg "Campbellock Jr." Pope, Bill "Slim the Robot" Williams, Toni Basil, and Fred "Rerun" Berry.

PAGE 90 An emulation of a basement house party, the *Soul Train* set was like home to every viewer. **TOP** Pat Davis. **MIDDLE LEFT** Damita Jo Freeman in 1974. **MIDDLE RIGHT** Adolfo "Shabba Doo" Quinones (right) down the *Soul Train* Line. **ABOVE** The Lockers.

> FRED BERRY WAS MOST RENOWNED FOR HIS ROLE AS RERUN ON THE TELEVISION HIT SHOW *WHAT'S HAPPENING!!*, WHERE HE'D SPONTANEOUSLY BUST OUT HIS BRAND OF LOCKING IN MOST ANY PLACE, FROM THE SCHOOL CAFÉ TO THE SODA SHOP.

ABOVE Don dancing down the Line with Mary Wilson in Episode 60 on May 12, 1973. **TOP RIGHT** Pam Brown (center) managed the dancers with kid gloves but adult rules. **BOTTOM RIGHT** Pam Brown's (center) tenure at *Soul Train* lasted as long as Don's.

The search began at a playground in Dinker Park in Los Angeles, and all the killer dancers were there. The kids had to be at least fifteen-years-old to participate, and they came in droves for a shot to blow the minds of anyone who would admire their taut bodies, chiseled facial features, artful hair, and courageous moves. The early auditions were cloaked in midwestern naïveté—Don described them as an introduction to beautiful people who were "just plain exciting to look at." He said that where he came from, the people who wanted to be on television should *never* be on television, but "LA contained every person in the world who wanted to be on television *and should be*." The glamour, invention, and creativity were refreshing and made him hopeful. That first wave of auditions knocked the producers out and gave Don the gift of developing the nucleus of his show.

At the same time, Don was offering the dancers something positive to engage in, and for many it was the first time they'd get "off the block" and meet new people. The vibe of the show was to encourage the dancers to be creative while requiring them to be responsible and accountable. Don stressed that how they dressed, spoke, acted, and looked would be the face of Afrocentricity that white America would see and judge, and that being a *Soul Train* Dancer meant being on the frontlines of it all. Therefore Don had rules. Rule number one: Follow the rules. Others included:

- No one under fifteen could audition for the show.
- No cussing, no negativity, no perverseness in dance or language, no disrespect, no attitude.
- No gym shoes, don't look sloppy.
- Be on time, be tactful, be creative, be funky, be yourself.
- Put your best foot forward.
- Have fun.

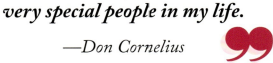

These are all my children. All very special people in my life.

—*Don Cornelius*

Don designated Pam Brown to manage the dancers, and she did just that for the entire thirty-five-year run of *Soul Train*, from 1971 to 2006. Her first day was the same as Don's first day. Pam was known as "that gum lady" because she thought nothing was less attractive than a kid on television chewing gum. Her no-gum rule became the most stringent rule of all. She worked at Dinker Park full time in addition to managing the dancers. She cared a lot about those kids and knew many of them, their temperaments, even where they lived. She would give a lift to the kids who might have missed the bus back to the train station. The parents knew that when their teenagers were on the set of *Soul Train* or with Pam, they were staying out of trouble.

The dancers quickly became mini-celebrities. They performed at public parks, were highlighted in school newspapers, and ventured into different neighborhoods to see what else was out in the world. As we watched them from our couches in Atlanta, Detroit, Philly, wherever, we got to venture outside our own bubbles, if only for an hour. In the dancers and the Scramble Board contestants, we met people from all over, with different ways of saying things, with dance moves unlike anything we'd seen. Instead of comparing and contrasting, or rivaling, we aimed to learn something from one another, whether a hair style, a favorite song, or what other kids did for kicks. Mostly we got to learn new dances.

The way it was before technology connected the world, you would go to Detroit and people would be dancing and talking one way, and then hit Chicago and see them do things that blew your mind, and then experience totally different flavors in Mobile, St. Louis, Miami, or New Orleans. When *Soul Train* became syndicated, people no longer danced in different ways in different regions—they danced like the kids on *Soul Train*.

RIGHT Choreographed moves and clothing were ubiquitous on *Soul Train*. **BELOW** Pulling stunts like the performer, Mr. X didn't need a name to be remembered. **OPPOSITE BOTTOM** The original superfly, Mr. X. **OPPOSITE RIGHT** The *Soul Train* Scramble Board.

TRAIN TRENDS

Soul Train Dancers were responsible for many iconic dance trends. Do you remember the first time your classmate did the Robot? He can thank Charles "Robot" Washington for that one. The Stop and Go by Damita Jo? And remember the Hustle, the Bump, the Bus Stop, the Backslide, the Reject, waacking, punking, tutting, popping? The Running Man? They might not have been invented on *Soul Train*, but *Soul Train* served as the vehicle to transform local, ingenious dance pioneers into decade-defining, international ones.

The *Soul Train* Line

Don said at first he resented the accusation that *Soul Train* was a second-rate *American Bandstand,* but once he really thought about it, that is exactly what it was. Except *Soul Train* was no sock hop. Don was clear that his dancers didn't get in just because they waited in line; they were chosen by Pam Brown because each possessed a talent and a look that the show encapsulated. This precision in getting the right people to dance on the show was partly rooted in Don's innate dancing ability. In Chicago's South Side, where Don grew up, a person's degree of coolness was wrapped up in how well he could dance. Wherever there was a party, Don was the one who would throw down, so it made sense that he brought this unbridled cool factor to televisions everywhere.

Don took the universally recognizable format of performance and dance in *American Bandstand* and added a whole new dimension with the *Soul Train* Line. Week after week everyone waited for the dancers to form the Line. You could sense them chomping at the bit, because soon it would be their turn to show how cool, how smooth, how unique, and how joyful they were.

Originally the *Soul Train* Line consisted of couples moving down the middle of a row of women and men, who parted like the Red Sea to witness the couple's choreographed synchronized moves and crazy coordinated fashions. Later, two *Soul Train* Lines were used, one for women and the other for men. This allowed for more room to dance and more focus on the dancer and his or her individuality.

For a brief time the *Soul Train* Line was featured in the first half of the show. But its instantaneous popularity prompted Don to use it as the penultimate segment of the hour, before the headliner's second song. Any broadcasting person knows that to keep viewers tuned in, there needs to be the promise of a grand finale. At my grandmother's house where my aunts and cousins were participating in their weekly family ritual of having their hair done, the *Soul Train* Line was their Ice Cream Man. My job was to scream down the staircase to Grandma's kitchen, "The *Soul Train* Line is next!"

The *Soul Train* Line only lasted the length of one song (about three minutes), but in that time, Don brought you a diverse world on its feet. And what that did was abolish the regionalism of ghetto America. Back then the country was much bigger than it is now. Whatever was happening on one side of the country, the other side would never know about. For instance, there was a way of life in the Northeast, its own style, lingo, and dance that other parts of the country weren't privy to. The same went for the Southeast and the Midwest. Each region spoke funny and looked funnier from coast to coast, but *Soul Train* bridged these gaps. Watching *Soul Train* inspired teens to move to LA to be on the show and display their slice of life. Dance and fashion amalgamated, and black people, regardless of location, began to think on one wavelength.

OPPOSITE Sharon Moore makes a classic hip-bump move down the Line. **BELOW** The *Soul Train* Line was prime real estate, and dancers knew how to work the moment, no matter how brief it was.

ABOVE Joe Tex and Damita Jo put on a show like no other.

Spotlight on Damita Jo

When Joe Tex pulled Damita Jo Freeman onstage exclaiming "I Gotcha" while performing the 1971 hit in Episode 27 on April 1, 1972, a star was born. She brought the song to life by dancing as if she were a mime—strumming her raised thigh like a guitar, moving her body mechanically as if she were a robot, and air kissing, teasing, and taunting Tex through strut-like movements. It was theater. Later, in Episode 176 on February 28, 1976, when Joe performed the same song, Damita Jo was part of the act, already on stage, choreographing microphone stand tosses back and forth with Tex.

Her range was fluid, mechanical, rigid, and graceful, all in one. Because she didn't wear crazy outfits or have some sort of gimmick, her dancing and authenticity shined. She didn't need a stage name, a hat, or a prop to do her thing.

Damita Jo invented dance moves with her partner, Jimmy "Scoo B Doo" Foster, including the Stop and Go, which she premiered in 1972 to "Slow Motion" by Johnny Williams. And when she jumped onstage with James Brown in Episode 49 on February 10, 1973, she worked "Super Bad" as if she had been on the professional circuit for years. You could see the Godfather of Soul turning to his band mates with an inquisitive look, asking, "Did you guys catch that?" Not once did he sing to the audience. He kept his eyes on Damita Jo, marveling at what she could do.

The camera was drawn to her as well, and she always found her way into the dance contest, winning the second year's contest. What is telling about the "sweet disposition" that Damita Jo was said to have was her gutsy leadership of fellow dancers. She fought for dancers' rights, and ultimately formed a small dancers' union to protect them.

That a young girl with no prior background in show business was performing on a nationally syndicated show with legends like James Brown and Joe Tex was astonishing. These were precisely the sort of life-changing opportunities and messages that Don and *Soul Train* offered an entire generation.

High Energy

The dancers set the tone, the mood, and the energy level of every show. Their enthusiasm for a guest and their reaction to a song, even how hard they danced, influenced how people felt on the other side of the TV. The dancers' reaction to the music could so powerfully influence viewers' opinions that I believe Don played less popular songs during the *Soul Train* Line to garner more support for them. This seemed most apparent to me as I rewatched Episode 12 on December 18, 1971, when the fun really began.

On Episode 12, Don's pals from Chicago, the Chi-Lites, Joe Tex, and the Originals were guests. It wasn't the performances of the three *Soul Train* staple acts that made the episode historical; it was the crowd that day. The studio seemed at fuller capacity than usual, and the audience truly became part of the show. The dancers were hootin' and hollerin', cheering on one another, and connecting each corner of the studio in a symbiotic rhythm that was a sight to see. There was so much energy that three *Soul Train* Lines organically formed. The dancers looked more like a community than a bunch of kids who wanted to dance to some grooves—at least that's how it looked from my seat. I felt more like a participant than a spectator, and that is ultimately what kept everyone coming back for more.

ABOVE Without VCRs and DVRs, we didn't dare blink while the *Soul Train* Line segment was on, for fear of missing the moves. **BELOW** As the camera panned, each dancer knew it was their time to shine.

From Street to *Saturday Night Fever*

In the process of revolutionizing the art of dance on television, *Soul Train* introduced a pioneering form of street dance. By Episode 26 on March 25, 1972, the Lockers had come into their own, and suddenly everybody wanted to lock. The original Lockers went on to enjoy outrageous success as choreographers, actors, singers, businesspeople, and creative consultants to music's A-list.

By 1977, disco had a stronghold on the country, so Don tried to adapt by inviting professional dancers on the show, including Lester Wilson and Michael Peters. Don also added dance-offs: having the dancers vote on which couple's routine was "finished." This was meant to quench the audience's thirst for the disco-style, partner-centric dancing popularized by *Saturday Night Fever*'s Tony Manero in 1977. In my opinion, one of the most successful *Soul Train* shows of this period was the Minnie Riperton memorial in Episode 303 on September 15, 1979, in which a professional dance couple danced in her honor to her song "Simple Things."

Stepping Out of Line

Before the homogenization of dance that happened during 1983, we had the pioneers of the *Soul Train* Line. Here are my top picks for the 1970s.

Wayne "Crescendo" Ward—Like so many of the Kids, Wayne didn't know what he wanted to do, but upon seeing the Kids dancing on *Soul Train,* he said, "That's it! That's what I want to do!" He credits *Soul Train* with saving him from gangs: "Thug, hood, homeless, whatever, they watched *Soul Train,* so if I met up with the Four Corner Hustlers, they recognized me from the show and actually gave me money to take a cab back to my neighborhood."

Patricia Davis—One could say Pat shares the title of First Lady of *Soul Train* with Damita Jo Freeman, even though Pat was officially voted "*Soul Train*'s Original All-Time Diva" by her peers at a dancer reunion. The camera panned the studio in search of her as much as it did for Damita Jo. While other dancers smiled and mouthed the lyrics to the songs they were moving to, Pat had a stoic look, one of intense focus that said, "I'm in the business of dancing." She often dressed her hair in oversized, colorful flowers and butterfly clips, inspired by Billie Holiday. Pat was breathtaking to watch down the *Soul Train* Line—as a rag doll, in a man-tailored suit, or as her showstopper self. She

> *Even Michael Jackson got a lot of his moves from watching* **Soul Train.** *There were not many places that Michael Jackson could go to get ideas about dancing.*

THIS PAGE The *Soul Train* Dance Contest in 1975 brought out the ingenious in contestants. Even little kids had their chance to get their game on. **OPPOSITE TOP** "Fluky Luke" Williamson with the Lockers. **OPPOSITE BOTTOM** Christina Sanchez marks the moment with her makeshift sign.

> IKE TURNER'S COUSIN QUEEN TURNER WAS A *SOUL TRAIN* DANCER, WHOSE PARTNER WAS EDDIE FRANKLIN, ARETHA FRANKLIN'S SON.

was the epitome of what black girls strived to be: oozing with soul. Oh, and she got to wipe the sweat off Marvin Gaye's forehead during "Let's Get It On."

Jimmy "Scoo B Doo" Foster—You had to feel bad for any dancer who went down the line with Scoo B, because you hardly noticed her, unless it was his legendary partner, Damita Jo, who was responsible for bringing him on the show. He was that good and intensely fun to watch. Already a member of the Lockers before joining the show, Scoo B was a master at making his long limbs extend even farther, like an X marking the spot across your TV set. He invented a slew of dances, including the Scoo B Doo, the Scoo-Bot, the Stop and Go, the Scoo B Hop, the Scoo B Kick, and the Scoo B Walk. And if his fluid movements and magnetic personality didn't make your lashes stick to your eyebrows, his rubber band–like jumps and splits and his sole-sliding manipulations would.

Thelma Davis—Thelma was one of the original members of the *Soul Train* Gang. Her dance style wasn't as flashy or flamboyant as that of some of the other dancers. Instead it was elegant and had a flair of trained control, as she spun with precision or danced ballroom style with her many partners. Thelma referred to herself as the "pass around girl" on the dance floor because she got bored easily. When a partner wanted to do the same routines and steps over and over again, she would move on to someone else, wanting to try something new. Dressed many times in a leotard, she looked like she was heading to a ballet bar right after the show.

Darnell Williams—Darnell, who hailed from London, gained fame after *Soul Train* starting in 1981 for his role as Jesse Hubbard on *All My Children*. (Before you get the wrong idea, take heart in the fact that my parents were still on their PBS kick then, so my fandom remained strictly related to his role on *Soul Train*.) He won Daytime Emmy Awards for that role.

Tyrone "The Bone" Proctor and Sharon Hill—Sharon was one of the prettiest and most energetic dancers to grace *Soul Train*. After Pat Davis urged Sharon to find herself a partner, she saw Tyrone practicing his moves and asked him to join her. So they got together and were asked to do a routine for the weekly dance contest. She and Tyrone

> SHARON MET HER HUSBAND, MARK WOOD OF THE R&B/FUNK GROUP LAKESIDE, THROUGH *SOUL TRAIN*.

THESE PAGES We tuned into *Soul Train* so we could show off our moves at parties. It's hard to imagine a world without *Soul Train* to provide an outlet for dancers like these.

did the P.A. Slaughter, which got them into the Los Angeles finals of the *Soul Train* dance contest. Their routines won each of them many fans across the country, and they became one of the show's most popular couples. They even won a dance contest on *American Bandstand*.

Lil' Joe Chism and Yolanda Seay—Lil' Joe and Yolanda were regular dance partners who did the Scramble Board and won a year's supply of Ultra Sheen and Afro Sheen products. Yolanda was a vibrant and terrific dancer as well as a fashionista. She smiled a lot, attracting viewers to her warm girl-next-door persona. Lil' Joe was known for smuggling dancers, including Jeffrey Daniel, into the studio, even though they were supposed to wait in line. I remember thinking Lil' Joe and Yolanda had to be nervous when they competed in the *Soul Train* Dance Contest, which was judged by Don and James Brown. However, Yolanda basically went down in lucky-girl history when Marvin Gaye sang "Let's Get It On." He pulled Yolanda out of the crowd and sang to her, and afterward she gave him a little kiss on the cheek.

Jermaine Stewart—Pal of Jeffrey and Jody on the dance floor, Jermaine was originally up for lead singer of the group Shalamar, but lost the part to Howard Hewett. Jermaine did, however, tour with the group and remained close with his fellow Chicagoan childhood friends in it, Jeffrey Daniel and Jody Watley. Later, Culture Club member Mikey Craig assisted Jermaine in making a demo and invited him to sing backup with the band until they helped him get a contract with Arista. The result: "You Don't Have to Take Your Clothes Off."

PATTI IS ONE OF A SELECT GROUP OF ARTISTS WHO ALWAYS INSISTED ON SINGING LIVE. WITH NINETEEN-PLUS PERFORMANCES, SHE HOLDS THE RECORD FOR HAVING HAD THE MOST LIVE PERFORMANCES OF ANY ACT IN THE SHOW'S HISTORY. OTHER LIVE PERFORMANCES INCLUDED ONES BY BARRY WHITE, AL GREEN, JAMES BROWN, THE J.B.'S, SLY & THE FAMILY STONE, AND TOWER OF POWER.

> *We had artists say they wouldn't lip-sync. We would either do it, or lose the booking. These [live shows] were the most exciting times of my whole life. I loved them that much.*
>
> —Don Cornelius

LEFT Labelle never failed to show up in the craziest ensembles. **RIGHT** Labelle even tricked out their Nikes. **BOTTOM** Labelle in Episode 118 on December 7, 1974.

104 SOUL TRAIN

LEFT Side Effect. **ABOVE** Jody Watley and Jeffrey Daniel were childhood friends and dance partners on *Soul Train*.

Focus on Fashion

Black artists discovered that it wasn't enough to perform material—they had to *entertain* their audiences. Visual presentation in a live setting proved crucial to those who would thrive in the 1970s and into the future. The London fashion scene had influenced the style of the 1960s in America, specifically the Bay Area. David Bowie's Ziggy Stardust persona proved mightily influential to both rock and soul audiences, giving them a limitless palette to work with. In my opinion, Labelle's Episode 118 on December 7, 1974, marked the beginning of a wave of outlandish futuristic costumes. Even though the Pointer Sisters also used theatrics, their references were to an older time. Labelle used costume and theater to reflect the unknown future.

Labelle came to perform their most popular hit, "Lady Marmalade," sung by Patti LaBelle. Labelle's performance elicited some of the loudest outbursts of excitement and praise, which during this period of *Soul Train* was quite the achievement, since the standards were already so high. In her nine appearances on the show, Patti never left the *Soul Train* audience underwhelmed.

Soon other bands stepped up their presentation game. Mandrill, the New Birth, Instant Funk, Jeffrey Daniel, the Trammps, Side Effect, Teddy Pendergrass, and Shalamar, among others, would baffle, humor, and sometimes haunt me.

Spotlight on Jeffrey and Jody

Probably the most famous dancers to come out of the show, Jeffrey Daniel and Jody Watley were proof of what happens when talent merges with opportunity. They were friends from church from the time Jody was a young teen. A young Jeffrey and Jody carpooled to *Soul Train* to dance their hearts out. They were accompanied by fellow Chicagoan and *Soul Train* dancer Jermaine Stewart.

Once Jeffrey and Jody achieved a notoriety and fan base, they began incorporating skits into their dances. A personal favorite of mine is Episode 197 on November 13, 1976 (Aretha Franklin and Ronnie Dyson), where they staged a faux brawl. I thought this was a stroke of genius and moments like these constantly kept me tuned to see what antics they would pull off next. Nobody expected it, and everyone thought it was real, even fellow dancer Tyrone Proctor, who broke up the fight by pulling them apart.

By Season 6 in 1976, the lack of set design and distractions allowed the power couple to shine even more. They began using different props, inciting the popular uses of Chinese fans, skateboards, pogo sticks, a unicycle, and umbrellas. They dressed in running gear, did aerobics, rolled on the ground—you name it.

Of course, what else would you expect from the guy who essentially taught Michael Jackson how to moonwalk, and the woman who would go on to become a Grammy Award–winning solo artist? How about joining a musical group, calling themselves Shalamar, and selling millions of albums worldwide over a seven-year period?

THE BIG MOMENTS

For me, the interviews between Don and his guests always let the genius out of the bottle. He used the interview segments for a variety of purposes. There were those fashioned as public service announcements, like when Stevie Wonder spoke about the importance of education or James Brown explained that black-on-black crime could not be tolerated. There was also flirty Don, who couldn't hide his crushes on female artists, including Bonnie Pointer. Every time Bonnie was in close proximity, even the eight-year-old me knew to yell at my television set, "Get a room." At other times, Don would run the risk of inciting sibling ire by giving a little too much attention to Bunny DeBarge or Joni Sledge. Even in the hottest moments, Don was so suave that he never lost his cool, no matter who the guest was. The one exception was Diana Ross; he admitted that she made him nervous. And even that admission represented its own kind of humanizing cool.

PAGE 106 Diana Ross makes a special guest appearance in Episode 55 on April 7, 1973. **TOP LEFT** Diana Ross had already broken from the Supremes by the time she met Don on the set of *Soul Train*. **TOP RIGHT** After the Rumble in the Jungle match, George Foreman comes in peace to *Soul Train* in 1974. **ABOVE** Billy Davis Jr. and Marilyn McCoo of the 5th Dimension talk with Don in Episode 87 on January 26, 1974.

In my opinion, *Soul Train* would have enjoyed only a five-to seven-year run had it not been for Don's professionalism and ability to communicate through the interviews. Having been on the show twice myself, I can attest that he was the epitome of coolness. The Roots' first episode, number 946, aired on March 4, 2000. Shemar Moore was hosting, since Don had retired from that side of the show six years before. But Don was still there writing, directing, and producing, and I heard him bragging, "I didn't have cue cards in my day." This completely shocked me. *How did he absorb all that text?* Simple, he didn't. He genuinely loved his baby and the artists who came to nurture it, so he exuded an air of absolute confidence. And he did his own research, another rarity in show business.

During some interviews, you met a side of Don you couldn't believe existed. I call it "locker room" Don. It was that guy's guy thing, and he only had it with certain people. Seeing the fatherly, authoritative Don let loose and talk straight up to a guest as if they had just finished a game of pickup, forgetting the audi-

ABOVE Cholly Atkins working with the O'Jays on their song "Give the People What They Want."

ence was there, was such a kick. That's why there was always an extra bonus whenever the show was visited by the Whispers, the Temptations, and *especially* the O'Jays. Don was the loosest during one of the most treasured moments—the famous basketball game between Don and Marvin Gaye, refereed by Smokey Robinson, on **EPISODE 222 ON MAY 7, 1977**. For me, this was one of the only good things that happened during *Soul Train*'s disco era.

Watching these segments now is so entertaining because I catch sexual innuendos, professional business tensions, and mutual respect that were lost on me as a child. For instance, minutes before the Supremes' Mary Wilson convinced Don to accompany her down the *Soul Train* Line in **EPISODE 60 ON MAY 12, 1973**, she asked him, "Don, can I dance with you?" Don replied, "Yes, but not on television." After a commercial break, the *Soul Train* line segment began, and toward the middle of the song, Don and Mary danced down the Line to "Doing It to Death" aka "Gonna Have a Funky Good Time" by the J.B.'s. This is a top ten alert, as it marks the only time Don danced down the Line. He certainly lived up to his South Side reputation. These were the moments that made everyone smile and feel like they were being invited into Don's world in a big way.

The O'Jays

The O'Jays' performances were consistently solid and crowd-pleasing. Their every appearance caused a frenzy among the female dancers because of Eddie Levert's emotive singing style. The personal chemistry that Don and Eddie shared brought a humorous backdrop to the show. And as incredible as the O'Jays performed, the banter between the two was the true highlight. Eddie helped bring out Don's humorous side, which was so integral to his persona.

Humor is a way to gain access to the third dimension of a stranger. With humor you get to see someone's vulnerable side because humor helps people relax. Don and Eddie's relationship was particularly notable because it was like watching two old friends talk and have fun on camera in front of millions of people. They would often "play the dozens," meaning they'd dig on one another, joking about a hit single or lack thereof, how one of them was too old, or not hip. In Episode 57 on April 21, 1973, Don invited Eddie to do an impersonation of him, one which Eddie had first showed off at a party they both attended in Cleveland.

For me, a big moment was when the O'Jays enlisted the talents of the incomparable Cholly Atkins, known for his

THE BIG MOMENTS

SMOKEY AND ARETHA

There's something to be said about a backstage glimpse of the blood, sweat, and tears that musicianship and entertainment require. But what makes **EPISODE 314 ON DECEMBER 1, 1979**, easily an iconic top ten moment of *Soul Train*, and perhaps in all of performance history, is the exact opposite. In a "Salute to Aretha Franklin," when Don facetiously challenged a young, pristine Aretha on whether she was "even old enough to know any of Smokey's music," she didn't flinch. Smokey's cackling reaction had that boys' club flavor I enjoyed so much between Don and his guests. A jab at the "old man" Smokey it was not. Sitting to the left on the piano bench next to her Detroit comrade Smokey, Aretha was expressionless until she bore the weight of her fingers onto the ivory keys and prayerfully cooed, "Ooo, baby baby."

Effortless. It was the exact opposite of the commendable rehearsing I'd seen Cholly Atkins do with the O'Jays. It was obviously the other side of the same talent coin. Aretha continued, "Ooo, baby baby." Like a cat to nip, Smokey rang in his falsetto, and they hypnotically fell into a melodious duet as if they had done it a million times. It was raw organic talent that needed no choreography or showmanship. The stuff legends are made of.

choreography of the Motown family. From the Supremes and the Four Tops to the Temptations, Cholly basically taught them how to dance, spending countless hours rehearsing. He helped define the Motown brand, as each act's package relied on choreography. Atkins also stepped outside the Motown circle and choreographed many other groups of the '60s era.

In the mid-'70s, the world of television had few frills, so even the slightest editing trick was enough to make my jaw drop. In Episode 153 on October 11, 1975, a behind-the-scenes tape aired showing Atkins working with the O'Jays on choreography for their song "Give the People What They Want." Cholly was counting the cadence, "1-2-3-4, 1-2-3-4," as the guys turned and stumbled over their feet. "Do it like you were on *Soul Train*," Cholly challenged them; and bam, the O'Jays were cleverly transformed into

OPPOSITE A duo worth dying for, Aretha and Smokey sing it out in Episode 314. **ABOVE** Billy Preston is magnetic in Episode 85 on January 5, 1974.

their show clothes and onto the *Soul Train* set, where they rolled right into the song, sans the typical introduction by Don. This raw look at what went into getting from point A (conception) to point B (polished and poised entertainers) added an entirely new dimension to what music, entertainment, and collaboration were all about. It showed how *Soul Train* continued to creatively strive to set new standards in television production and avoid becoming stale while giving the people what they wanted (before they knew they wanted it).

The Fifth Beatle

Similar to Ike and Tina, Billy Preston wasn't deemed a soul act just because of the color of his skin. He was rock 'n' roll royalty and had more white fans than black. But Billy, gospel born and soul bred in his bones, arrived to *Soul Train* acknowledging that he was one of our own. He was not your average piano-playing, singing guy; and Don made certain to say so, establishing for his viewership that this man was a legend, "the fifth Beatle." I was proud of Don for the reverence with which he treated Billy.

The Isley Brothers

I honor Chuck Berry and Little Richard as the father and architect, respectively, of rock 'n' roll, but I will say that the Isley Brothers on Episode 119 on December 14, 1974, had an almost hypnotic effect on the *Soul Train* Kids. This was most notably because of the youngest brother, Ernie Isley, who spent his

THE BIG MOMENTS

childhood hiding in a closet spying on frequent stowaway and unofficial family member James Marshall Hendrix as he practiced his left-handed guitar.

After the army honorably discharged him for "unsuitability" in 1962, Jimi Hendrix cut his teeth in the R&B grind doing stints with Little Richard. The last group he worked with before he became Jimi Hendrix was the Isley Brothers. They took him into their New Jersey home from the streets of Greenwich Village. While he was practicing his skills, Ernie was eleven or twelve years old, and he observed Jimi's every move and then practiced what he saw. And quiet as it is kept, the baton was passed to Ernie when Jimi passed in 1970.

People often think that Jimi's music found its way into George Clinton's P-Funk universe, but I don't think any group had its feet planted in traditional R&B's past and psychedelic rock's future better than the Isley Brothers. And this episode demonstrates it well: they are live, and they are loud. The band let Ernie take over the show, picking up where Jimi left off—playing with his teeth, lying on his back on the floor. For a black America that, like me, didn't know any better, he looked like the pioneer of this stuff. The episode is one of my personal favorites because I had never seen showmanship like this in my life. It is also a historical pick because it established that the Isleys would experience a third decade of success. They grew from a doo-wop act into a futuristic funk rock hybrid. It was a reinvention that most acts could only dream of.

Average White Band and the Undisputed Truth

Episode 161 on December 6, 1975, featured Average White Band and the Undisputed Truth. This is the first time that the *Soul Train* audience got to see a white band transposed in a black tradition. Even Don's introduction noted the novelty of Average White Band: "Here is an act that must be seen to be believed. A group so funky you'd swear that they were raised on collard greens, black-eyed peas, and ham hocks, even though they were raised in the UK."

This was when I stopped trying to be a Bill Withers wannabe guitarist and decided to become a Steve Ferrone–like drummer. Average White Band played live on the show, and instantly I said to myself, *That's my instrument*. It was important for them to play live, because without the use of video, America would not have believed who was making a sound so authentically black. Steve, who had just joined the band, was the only African American member. Everyone had seen white acts redo rock 'n' roll and doo-wop, and play jazz and Bach, but to approximate funk was probably the blackest expression a performer could make.

ABOVE The Undisputed Truth in Episode 161 on December 6, 1975.
OPPOSITE The Isley Brothers in Episode 119 on December 14, 1974.
LEFT There's nothing average about Average White Band in Episode 161 on December 6, 1975.

Add to this episode the second appearance by the Undisputed Truth, a band pigeonholed as a gender-mixed group like the 5th Dimension and Hues Corporation, which were not as popular as unisex groups like the Temptations or the Supremes. At the time, they didn't stand out as much as those groups, despite their '70s hit "Smiling Faces." On the *Soul Train* stage, though, they came out wearing silver makeup, white wigs, and platform shoes—a crazy cosmic motif. Along with the New York Dolls, David Bowie, and Funkadelic, their outer space shtick proved to be a reinvention for the ages. I remember Don's reaction during the interview: he was a little weirded out. I think this was because they had looked so normal in Episode 16 three years earlier.

THE BIG MOMENTS

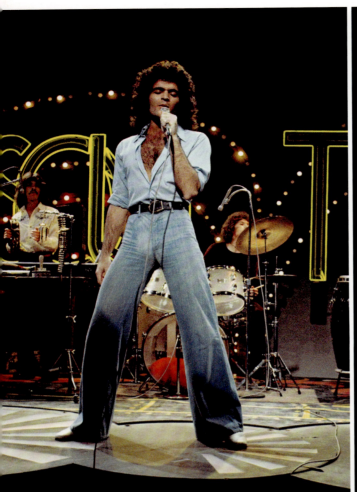

ABOVE LEFT Gino Vannelli, a Canadian signed to the A&M label, stood out for being the first white vocalist on *Soul Train* in Episode 128 on February 15, 1975. His style was jazz and progressive rock, closer to the music of Weather Report than James Brown. **ABOVE RIGHT** José Feliciano in Episode 120 on December 21, 1974.

Trifecta

Episode 120 on December 21, 1974, showcased a headliner, a supporting act, and a guest act that each hit the bull's-eye—José Feliciano, Minnie Riperton, and the Dynamic Superiors.

In the first act of this rare trifecta, Feliciano's singing was on fire, which was important for indicating how people from other cultures embraced the show. The Puerto Rican singer from Spanish Harlem stunned the audience with a fiery performance of "Hard Times in el Barrio," a cover of Stevie Wonder's "Golden Lady," and a striking version of "California Dreamin'" by the Mamas & the Papas.

Not to be outdone, Minnie, in her five-and-a-half-octave glory, demonstrated her dexterity with "Lovin' You" and "Reasons," as if they were walks in the park. I remember her performances because she looked just like she does on her album cover, and at the very end of "Reasons" she replicated the sound of a chirping bird. Mortals would have to whistle to reach that high a note, and when Don asked her if she had a golden larynx, Minnie shrugged it off. I had never heard a human being sing that high before, so to watch someone sing notes that you had thought up to that point were whistles was thrilling.

The third act, the Dynamic Superiors from Washington, DC, put on one of *the* finest near Baryshnikov-level choreographed performances I've ever seen, with "Shoe Shoe Shine." You would think there isn't much you could do with such a slow melody, but the precision required to keep pace with the ballad is precisely what made the choreography complex. Their moves were exacting and in sync, as they used up most of the floor space to showcase their blend of tapping soles and sweeping footwork.

HISTORIANS NOTE THAT THEY COULD HEAR THE SOUNDS OF MINNIE RIPERTON'S THEN TWO-YEAR-OLD DAUGHTER, MAYA RUDOLPH, OFF STAGE.

TRIBUTE TO MINNIE RIPERTON

In July 1979, Minnie Riperton passed away from breast cancer. I was eight years old, and yet the gravitas of the moment was clear. The "Tribute to Minnie Riperton," in Episode 303 on September 18 of that year, made me sad. I was used to *Soul Train* being a jovial, celebratory environment, and the dimly lit set made it clear that this was an occasion for mourning. The highlight was an unannounced performance by Stevie Wonder. And even his demeanor was a little *too* somber. Stevie's previous performances had shared the motif of him sitting next to Don at the piano, singing impromptu songs. That wasn't the case this time. Stevie revealed, even though most suspected, that he was the producer of Minnie's *Perfect Angel* album. The album credits include "El Toro Negro" (The Black Bull). Everyone knew Stevie is a Taurus and black.

On the episode, Don and Stevie spoke softly to one another. Don said, "You wrote and produced this record." "Yeah, I was there. I helped," replied Stevie, his voice cracking. He told stories of how he was obsessed with Minnie, how he had been a fan of her previous group, Rotary Connection, and how when he first met her, he begged her to let him produce her music. It was a sad moment, and as I watched with my grandfather and cousin, I felt the historical significance.

LEFT Minnie Riperton in Episode 120 on December 21, 1974.
ABOVE Minnie Riperton.

THE BIG MOMENTS

BRINGING THE BLUES

The recurring theme for the top ten moments on *Soul Train* is, for the most part, that they were spontaneous moments. When it comes to off-the-top-of-the-head, freestyle wizards, B. B. King, Bobby Bland, and James Brown occupy that street. Is there any form of music that embodies the spirit of visceral impromptu music better than the blues? **EPISODE 132 ON MARCH 15, 1975**, was another one of those teachable moments, where you saw all three trading off-the-cuff lyrics like well-seasoned jazz musicians. Don's nod to the blues legends was an act of commemorating the African American culture, humbling us all with the reality check that even on the eve of the hedonistic disco era, the need to sing the blues might never be too far away.

TOP 10 ALERT

ABOVE Elton John in Episode 121 on May 17, 1975. **LEFT** B. B. King (left), James Brown (middle), and Bobby Bland (right).

Elton John

When Elton John appeared in Episode 141 on May 17, 1975, the show reached its summit, both visually and culturally. His outfit made him look like the leprechaun in my Lucky Charms morning cereal, and his appearance underscored the feverish reputation *Soul Train* had achieved. By this time, established pop stars like Elton were vying to get on the show. Elton had told Don that he was a fan, using the unfortunate phrase of being "amused by the show." Nonetheless, when Elton's people reached out to *Soul Train* for a booking, Don rolled out the red carpet.

By 1974, Elton had enjoyed two years of massive fame in the States after he hit the *Billboard* chart with "Rocket Man (I Think It's Going to Be a Long Long Time)," "Crocodile Rock," and "Daniel," and reached glam rock status after his *Goodbye Yellow Brick Road* album gave the world several more hits. Elton's arrival was a spectacle, and Don went to the ends of the earth to ensure it was nothing short of spectacular. Only certain dancers were allowed to be on the show, and Elton was permitted to sing live and bring along his custom plexiglass piano.

Performing "Bennie and the Jets" and "Philadelphia Freedom" in his glorious glittered eyewear, Elton was a natural fit—an English pop sensation with soulful overtones. The dancers reacted to Elton by mouthing and singing along. The episode was an important moment for cultural relations. It stated to me that if your music was quality, you would be embraced by *Soul Train*. Talent transcends all, no matter what color you are. Elton was a prime example.

David Bowie

Botched lip-syncing aside, I loved Bowie's performances of "Golden Years" and "Fame" in Episode 165 on January 3, 1976. Funky and cool, both songs were well received by the Kids, and Bowie's grooves coupled with his superlative persona and quality sense of humor called attention to the elephant in the room—that it was impossible to lip-sync songs with special effects like the ones in "Fame." So what did the guy do? Well, near the end of his song, he stopped and stood staring at the microphone. Then he flicked it as if to say, "Is this thing on?"

Don introduced him as "one of the world's most popular and important music personalities," and began the interview. Bowie plugged his film *The Man Who Fell to Earth,* as well as his upcoming world tour, and told Don that he hoped Russia would allow him to play there. Bowie was nothing but gracious and enthusiastic to be on the show, and the audience members seconded a congratulatory comment made by one of the Kids during the Q&A segment, applauding him for "getting into soul music." To me, he looked surprised, as though he hadn't thought of it like that. The Kids and Don accepted Bowie because he was the real deal—a multifaceted star from across the pond. His music was just plain good. Surpassing color, gender, age, genre, and hometown, talent and the sound of one's music is what really matters.

The End of the Decade

An entire decade had been defined by an intrepid man with a novel idea, but that is not to say *Soul Train* didn't equally benefit from what the decade had to offer it. A perfect give-and-take that was at the right place at the right time, *Soul Train* in the 1970s answered a community's search for a rainbow behind a hovering dark cloud of grief, loss, and hopelessness. It took a man who was in love with dancing and music to bring a celebration of Afrocentricity into everyone's living rooms. In a short amount of time, a show that couldn't attract the "big acts" was not only turning down the soul royalty of the '50s and '60s as well as the current trendsetters of the '70s, it went on to discover and nurture its own acts.

An empire had been built in what seemed like a day, and now it was time to say goodbye to free-bird dance grooves, overgrown Afros, chitlin circuits, five-man Motown singers, and supergroup sensations. Throughout the early '80s, familiar faces still dropped by the *Soul Train* stage, but eventually a new era took over that would transform Don Cornelius's dream and take it to a whole new level.

BOTTOM With a decade behind him and many top ten moments under his belt, Don certainly had something to smile about.

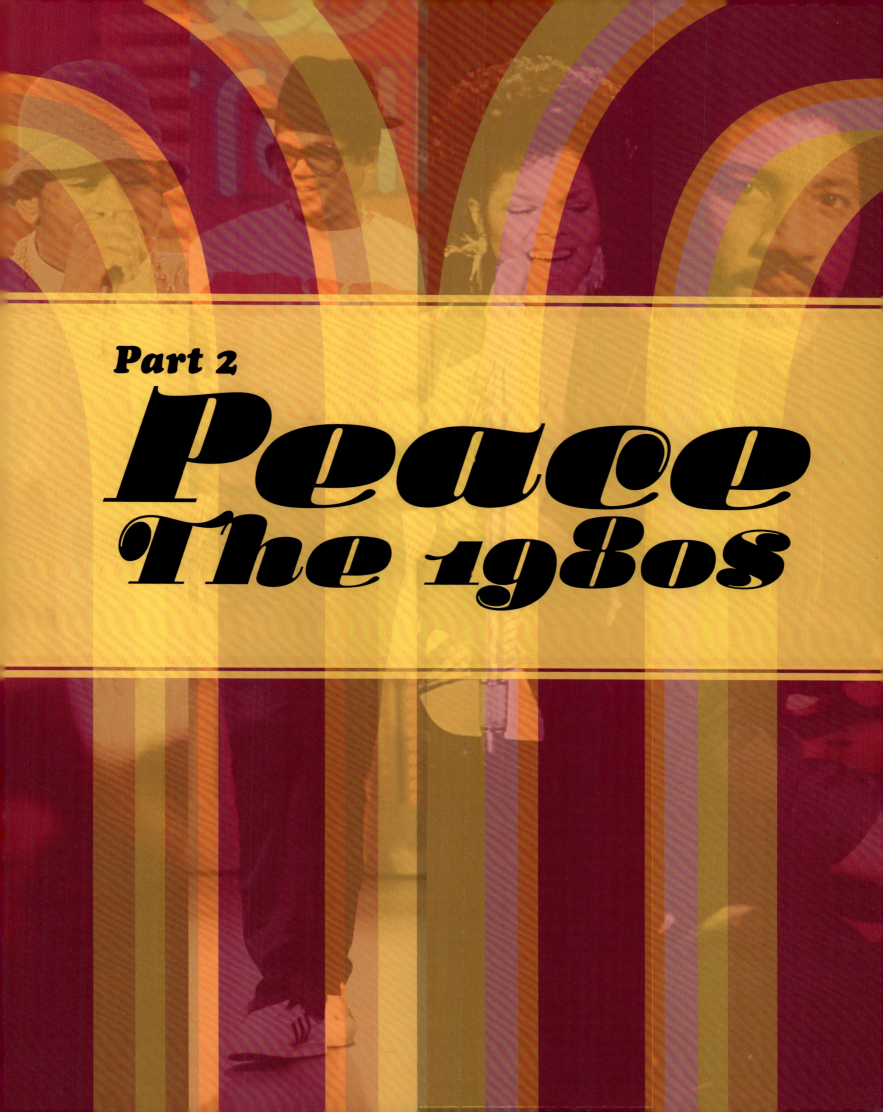

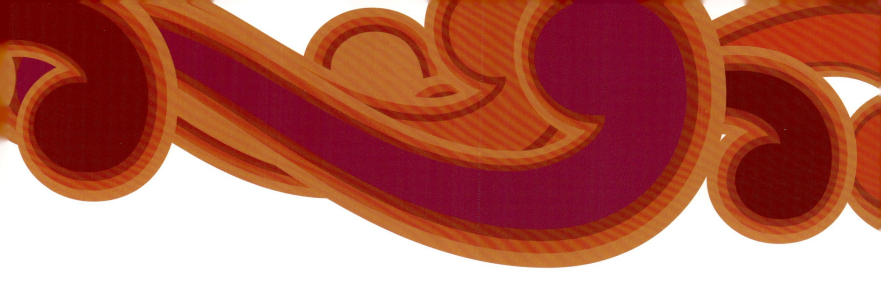

THE IDEA

The 1980–1981 season was *Soul Train*'s tenth, and it was apropos that Kurtis Blow ushered in the decade by presenting an entirely new musical genre, performing "The Breaks" while wearing a suit jacket and no shirt. Clap your hands everybody, if you've got what it takes. The appearance, kinetic and exciting, instantly made Don Cornelius look like a visionary, when in actuality he harbored considerable skepticism of this new music, which some people called hip-hop. Don had been uncertain once before, about disco music, and that time he had been right to be uncertain: its life span ended up being about as long as a one-term presidency. He may have sensed that hip-hop was a little different. In the interview, he explained to Kurtis in no uncertain terms that while he didn't share the kids' enthusiasm for hip-hop, he knew he had to "deal with it." And, man, did he deal with it.

PAGE 120 The set and dancers in 1984. **LEFT** Don Cornelius at his podium at the commencement of the 1980–1981 season. **BOTTOM** McFadden & Whitehead in Episode 310 predicted the future of the '80s on November 3, 1979, with "Ain't No Stoppin' Us Now." **ABOVE** Don between takes in Season 17 (1987–1988).

> *We wanted to make each show evolve into a shocking moment.*
>
> —Don Cornelius

Aside from being indicative of the shrewd moves Don made to keep the show on its heels, the Kurtis Blow show, Episode 336 on September 27, 1980, underscores how unflappable Don was during the interview process. This wasn't the first time Don had been met with cultural differences on the stage, but he never let his personal opinions affect an interview. Whatever he thought about the hip-hop genre, it did not filter through his cool demeanor as he spoke with Kurtis after his performance of "The Breaks."

Once the '80s came around, the flood of the disco era receded to reveal some dry land. Beginning with Season 10, the show was given a fresh start, and even though the producers embraced more funk-affirming styles like boogie, hip-hop, and go-go, *Soul Train* was considered less for its cultural significance and more for its showcase of great music and dance. So gone were the days of learning Swahili for "black is beautiful," and the hair commercials no longer taught you lessons about natural beauty. Now the products were geared toward how to blend into American society, like the ones for Jheri curl. It could tame an Afro and transform African American hair into a glossy and curled look that resembled a perm, which had become all the rage.

When Michael Jackson's video for "Don't Stop 'Til You Get Enough" premiered, the nation gasped. We spent the whole video trying to figure out what had happened to Michael's Afro. Michael was the first iconic music figure to drastically change his hair. I originally saw the video on Episode 307 in Season 9, and it

ABOVE Lakeside and the Whispers with Don in 1987.

blew my mind because I didn't know what to call his new hair. It wasn't a haircut, but it was wet and drippy looking. I remember that night I got my grandmother's Dippity Do, used the entire bottle, and went to church the next day with a DIY Jheri curl. (My parents would never let me get a real one.)

Now that the civil rights period was clearly over and the "me decade" had ended, all that was left was a proverbial piece of the pie up for grabs by everybody. Elevating oneself was priority number one. A friend of mine once stated that the most significant song of this period was "Ain't No Stoppin' Us Now" by McFadden & Whitehead because it was a song about upward mobility. But it also was about us not losing our way, not losing sight of the civil rights movement. The big message, to me, was: now that we have justice, let's achieve.

From boogie to hip-hop to new jack swing to rap, the '80s were a lot to keep up with, but Don proved that he was better under pressure, producing *Soul Train*'s most pinnacle years. This is my favorite period of the show's existence, particularly Seasons 14 through 17 (1984–1988), with Season 14 being the best of all. It really did not get better than this. I was obsessed.

Kicking and Screaming

By the time 1984 arrived, it was no wonder I was so entranced. I was relieved to see Don finally put the train in full throttle, because back in 1982 I had sensed the future of *Soul Train* was up in the air and that Don had been unsure of what direction to go. By hosting throwback acts like Edmund Sylvers, Lenny Williams of Tower of Power, the Stylistics, the Chi-Lites, the Bar-Kays, Rufus, Billy Preston, and a double booking of Shalamar and Lakeside (within thirteen episodes of each other), Don was digging in his heels against the new music era while remaining loyal to the groups who got him there in the first place.

Episode 385 with Mary Wells on April 10, 1982, comes to mind in particular. Don's sense of loyalty shined through, and by booking her he conveyed that he was not quick to dismiss an act that might be perceived as past its prime. Mary was then about to turn thirty-nine years old and had given Motown its first hit with "My Guy" eighteen years previous. She was considered a pioneer, as was Bettye LaVette, whom Don booked for Episode 387, a showcase of support for a veteran blues singer who was given a second lease on her career.

THE IDEA | **123**

TOP Bettye LaVette in Episode 387 on April 24, 1982. **ABOVE** Mary Wells comes to *Soul Train* in Episode 385 on April 10, 1982. **RIGHT** Smokey Robinson in Episode 556 on January 16, 1988. **OPPOSITE UPPER** Shalamar were already old pros by Episode 343 on November 15, 1980. **OPPOSITE LOWER** O'Bryan in Episode 447 on May 26, 1984.

Tribute to Smokey Robinson

What says loyal to the good old days better than a tribute to Smokey Robinson? And who else deserves a salute other than a man who was still making hits in the '80s, almost three decades after he began as the lead singer of the Miracles in the '50s? Smokey always had a coolness about him that didn't make him seem like someone of my parents' generation. Kids liked him, and he translated well into the '80s with his massive 1981 hit "Being with You," and later comeback hits, "Just to See Her" and "One Heartbeat," released in 1987, the year he was inducted into the Rock and Roll Hall of Fame.

Keep Moving or Die

Historically for *Soul Train*, the changes in music and culture in the 1980s weren't as radical as those from the era in which Elvis thrusted for the first time. But while the birth of the hip-hop movement did draw a line in the sand that divided generations, there was even more going on in music evolution—the very business of music was changing.

The year 1980 was when Black Entertainment Television (BET) debuted. With the introduction of a cable channel focused on African American viewers, *Soul Train* definitely lost the edge it had as the only game in town. *Soul Train* could never be what it wasn't; Don always planned to keep it a clean-cut weekly show. BET, on the other hand, was on cable two hours a week and appealed to a demographic that was more experimental and in search of ways of breaking ties from their parents' generation.

But Don didn't run scared just yet. I imagine he found solace in the fact that back in 1973 Dick Clark had tried to enter the soul market with a more risqué, controversial version of *Soul Train* called *Soul Unlimited,* hosted by actor Buster Jones. The show imploded after only a few episodes. One way that Don did feel a threat was the philosophy of 24/7 visual music, the revolutionary concept of making *The Midnight Special* weekly video approach a continual stream of music television, popularized by cable's Music Television (MTV). But he didn't seem to sweat it since, at the time, MTV was still picky about which black artists were featured on the air with videos (most were just "too black"), which meant Don continued to corner the African American market.

When MTV launched in 1981 and revolutionized the broadcasting of pop music with the help of Michael Jackson (who in turn revolutionized MTV), music videos proved to be the direction of the future. They offered visuals to beloved radio songs, and sensing this, Don figured he should catch the wave and perch himself on the crest.

The very first video on *Soul Train* actually dates back to Episode 158 on November 15, 1975, when supergroup War was

the special guest and they showed their title track, "Why Can't We Be Friends?" After that, music videos became an alternative way for an artist to appear on the show without having to perform in person. By Season 12, Don was playing more videos of former *Soul Train* regulars who had become too big to appear on the show, like Stevie Wonder, as well as acts that never quite made it on before they exploded into stardom, like Prince. Still, Don featured videos sparingly, using the twenty-minute mark of the show to either host dance contests or a new segment called "*Soul Train* History Book." The idea behind this "historical" bit was to showcase clips from the first four seasons; but by Season 13 in 1983, which happened to be the same year BET became a full-fledged 24/7 cable network, Don exclusively committed this segment to showing music videos and dropped the history theme altogether.

If this wasn't enough change to navigate with finesse, Don would outdo himself by solidifying control over a rapidly changing music market by creating protégés of his own. After Don and Dick Griffey dissolved their partnership in Soul Train Records in 1977, they both went their separate ways in music. Don discovered talent managing his own protégé, O'Bryan, whose funk, new wave, and rock elements were featured on his first album with Capitol Records. His single "The Giglo," peaked at number ten on the *Billboard* R&B chart in 1982. Dick Griffey hired Leon Sylvers III of the Sylvers to be his producer for the newly christened Solar Records, giving us such acts as the Whispers, Shalamar, Lakeside, and even Dick's wife, Carrie Lucas. Through Leon's production, there was the ability to forge the sound on the show in which there were disco overtones with more of a funk perspective. Generally, disco had become a neutered, numb-sounding, cocaine-fueled soundtrack for Studio 54—background music for a hedonistic lifestyle. Leon probably made the most significant change to disco by bringing it back to earth, terra firma, to its funk roots. Shalamar and, most notably, the Whispers, between 1979 and 1983, found success with this revised sound, until Prince made the last definitive statement on black music before hip-hop took over.

This move brought several changes in music. The first being the death of the supergroup. No longer did you need three guitarists, a horn section, or percussion, when a person like Kurtis Blow could show up and create the same sound with just one keyboard. Stevie Wonder had set the precedent by mastering new textures and synthesizers, which had awed folks back in the day, but which rapidly became the standard of the new decade. A lot of the established stars of the '70s were afraid of technology, and it was the death of many of their careers. Virtually everything could now be done on a keyboard.

On the flip side, you also had the manifestation of the "there's no stopping us now" attitude with '70s bands looking to hit pay dirt in the '80s, like Kool & the Gang and the Pointer Sisters. Other artists ditched their '70s bands to go solo, à la Lionel Richie, Dennis Edwards, Philip Bailey, Michael McDonald, Jeffrey Osborne, Ray Parker Jr., Bonnie Pointer, and Jody Watley, who reintroduced themselves during the decade, making *Soul Train* their vehicle for campaigning for their next musical regime. Even Michael Sembello left Stevie Wonder's band Wonderlove to write and perform one of the most definitive songs of the '80s, "Maniac," for the *Flashdance* soundtrack. He wowed the *Soul Train* dancers in Episode 427 on November 12, 1983. His fellow *Flashdance* comrade, Irene Cara, inspired the house with "Fame" in Episode 383 on March 27, 1982.

RIGHT Still two years away from busting ghosts, Ray Parker Jr. visits *Soul Train* in Episode 388 on May 1, 1982. **MIDDLE LEFT** A theme song sweetheart and sensation, Irene Cara in Episode 337 on October 4, 1980. **MIDDLE RIGHT** Irene Cara had achieved more than "Fame" by Episode 383 on March 27, 1982. **BOTTOM** Michael Sembello caught up with Don in Episode 427 on November 12, 1983 **OPPOSITE** A solo Watley in Episode 525 on December 27, 1986.

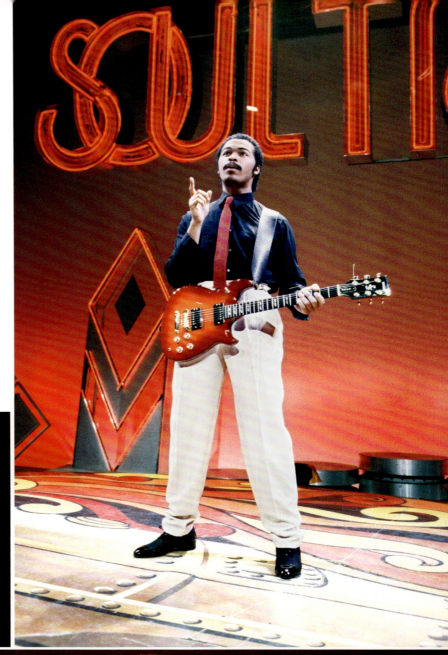

A New Genre and a New Jackson

Made popular by Anita Baker, retro nouveau R&B music became a gathering place for those who didn't make the transition to crossover stardom like James Ingram, Luther Vandross, Billy Ocean, Natalie Cole, Johnny Mathis, Stephanie Mills, Marilyn McCoo, Freddie Jackson, and Dionne Warwick, who was given her own tribute show in Episode 444 on May 5, 1984.

During this period, Don also had to contend with the triumphant solo career of Michael Jackson, who wouldn't be back on *Soul Train* in the '80s, and so set off in search of his next Jackson darlings—Jermaine and Janet. Little sister's 1982 debut album was produced by Foster Sylvers and René & Angela for A&M Records, which was indicative of how networking and good relationships helped Don stay on top of future hits across all genres. Janet appeared on *Soul Train* to promote her album that very same year as the support act to Michael McDonald in Episode 408 on December 18, 1982.

PAGES 128–129 The now-famous frontman steers his own ship in Episode 403, "Salute to Lionel Richie," on November 13, 1982. **TOP** Anita Baker in Episode 519 on November 15, 1986. **LEFT** By Episode 539 on May 30, 1987, Natalie Cole had carved out her niche. **ABOVE** James Ingram's place in the '80s is made known in Episode 380 on January 16, 1982. **RIGHT** Billy Ocean in Episode 616 on November 25, 1989. **OPPOSITE** The Romantics in Episode 448 on June 9, 1984.

JANET JACKSON

Donning a Dorothy Dandridge (or Hamill, take your pick) haircut, the shoulder-pad blouse, suspenders, and animal cage key that hung from her left earring, Janet was introduced by Don as "one of the most talented young ladies in show business . . . she now appears headed straight to the top as a singing recording artist." She went on to sing "Young Love," but admitted in her interview with Don that her first love was acting, as she was still playing Charlene on the television show *Diff'rent Strokes*.

Janet's sophomore appearance in Episode 458 on November 10, 1984 was to promote her album *Dream Street* and her being a regular on TV show *Fame*. It was an attempt to spark fireworks, but it wasn't until her third appearance two years later in Episode 498 that we got a glimpse of a determined, shrewd performer who clearly set out to present herself as a woman who was in control. It was March 1936 and her album *Control* had just been released. In walks Janet with hair to the sky. Her girl-next-door charm had been replaced by an age-appropriate scowl that reeked of teenage angst. She and her two male backup dancers turned out a choreography that made me sweat, while she seemed to be asking me right through the television "What Have You Done for Me Lately?"

When it comes to female solo performances on *Soul Train*, no one had seen a woman take over the room like Janet did. The studio audience could not calm down after Janet got through antagonizing and pouncing on them like a hunting black panther. Even Don was astonished; "Honey, you looked like you were gonna dig a hole in the stage," Don told her. "You look just like . . . Michael Jackson . . . whoever *that* is."

Without a doubt, Janet had arrived, kicked butt, taken names, and left people begging for more. Confident and energetic, she was seemingly in love with the music she was now producing. It was inevitable that her star status would soon rise far beyond even Don's *Soul Train* solar system. Miss Janet would not be back—ever.

LEFT Janet Jackson, still in love with acting, talks with Don in Episode 408 on December 18, 1982. **BELOW** Janet is in full-on singer-dancer mode in Episode 498 on March 26, 1986.

From Funk to Pop

Like Kool & the Gang and the Pointer Sisters, Atlantic Starr began urban and ended up pop. A nine-member funk band from upstate New York, they had by the early '80s managed to survive the storm of disco of the late '70s and landed in great boogie territory, especially with their lead singer Sharon Bryant, a soulful vocalist. When Sharon made her exit in 1985, she was replaced by Barbara Weathers, and it was Barbara's tenure with the band that would help them achieve their greatest pop successes.

Episode 498 on March 29, 1986, was a defining moment for Atlantic Starr, as they reintroduced themselves with a new lead singer, an adult contemporary sound, and a hit single in "Secret Lovers." This is notable because most funk bands were trying to adjust to the ever-changing atmosphere and ongoing metamorphoses of soul music. Whereas groups like the Pointer Sisters and Cameo could fit into a pop format with little damage to their established reputations, it was hard for Atlantic Starr to adjust to what was clearly going to wind up being the new reality for funk music, which meant incorporating hip-hop into the mix. So instead they went the opposite direction and found their zone in churban-adult contemporary ballad format.

Atlantic Starr continued to show off their new music sensibility in Episode 546 on October 10, 1987, when they performed the title cut off their first platinum album, "All in the Name of Love." The band said to Don in the interview in response to his congratulatory remarks on the album, "Yeah, it was a long time coming." Atlantic Starr went all the way to the bank as "balladeers."

TOP LEFT Freddie Jackson in Episode 551 on November 14, 1987. **ABOVE** An engaged Dionne Warwick takes questions from the audience in her tribute show in Episode 444 on May 5, 1984. **TOP RIGHT** Atlantic Starr became Atlantic shooting stars by Episode 498 on March 29, 1986.

Welcome Back to the Future: Take One

In 1982, Don remarkably survived an aneurysm and brain tumor at the age of forty-six. His condition kept him off the show for four months, but during this "break," Don ordered a brand-new, retooled show upon his return. In the middle of Season 12, in April 1983, he launched the refreshed show, managing to keep iconic classic elements so that it wasn't a total reinvention. A whole new set was built, and a new theme song written—which is my favorite of the eleven—along with the creation of a new sophisticated opening sequence and commercial bumpers, which were computer animated.

Episode 411 on April 30, 1983, boasted the Bar-Kays and O'Bryan, and both acts are very special to me, as it was this episode that unveiled a *Soul Train* with a stepped-up production game that said the show had officially entered the '80s and was no longer the "little train that could" of the '70s. The show had new dancers who embraced the b-boy culture, the fusion of popping, locking, and break dancing. Don now, in a non-ironic sense, fully embraced the bands from the new British invasion and straight-up pop groups. Groups like Duran Duran, the Romantics, Spandau Ballet, A-ha, and the Pet Shop Boys found a welcome home right next to Johnny Taylor, the O'Jays, the Commodores, and the Temptations.

The theme song before the launch of the redesign had remnants of disco. The new one, called "Soul Train's a Comin'," was the closest you could get to a hip-hop-groove-new-wave cross at the time. It was a slower funk song, penned by Don's protege, O'Bryan. And for the first time, the animated train finally danced in the same rhythm as the theme song, and I appreciated that the animators had painstakingly coordinated it all.

The production seemed more professional than ever, keeping up with the times without feeling cheesy. A lot of computer technology was used: up-to-date graphics, better camera angles and cuts, and a digital floating box—which showcased the artist of the day simultaneously with Sid McCoy's introduction. It gave the show a futuristic look, and it provided a sense of drama on top of an already suspense-filled Sid McCoy voiceover. With the stage dark and bright colors eliminated, it looked like the show fancied itself a nightclub. Seeing the dancers go down the Line as if they were at New York's Limelight club instead of a television studio was exciting.

Welcome Back to the Future: Take Two

Never one to be patient with a theme, at the beginning of Season 13 Don upped the ante again and gave the set another facelift, which debuted on October 15, 1983. The set had more lights than ever and used exaggerated digital technology, and the dance floor now looked more like an electronic city. While MTV had embraced loud fluorescent colors, *Soul Train* made use of its birth colors, shades of red and gold, going back to the feeling of classic *Soul Train* (1973–1975) but filtered through an '80s lens.

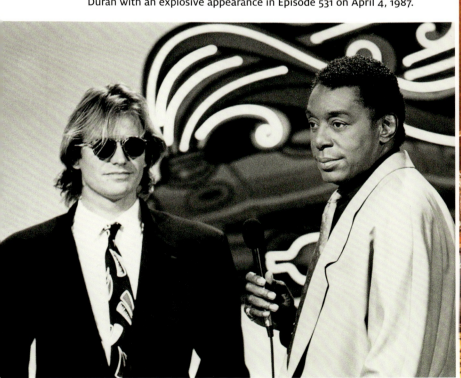

BELOW The gravitas hit the fan when the Zenist cat from across the pond, Sting, showed up in Episode 552 on November 21, 1987. **RIGHT** Duran Duran with an explosive appearance in Episode 531 on April 4, 1987.

Don also remixed O'Bryan's "Soul Train's a Comin'". Not since the "TSOP" theme of '73–'74 had *Soul Train* had a better intro song, which is pretty much a big reason why Season 13 is my favorite season of all time. "Soul Train's a Comin'" isn't the most iconic theme of the show or easily remembered, but in so much as musical direction goes, here we see funk infused at a time when it was becoming increasingly difficult to make your mark in that world. In my opinion, the Season 13 theme song was executed perfectly in its funkiness without having been influenced by anything of its type. It didn't sound like a Michael Jackson song; it didn't sound like a Prince song. It didn't sound like disco. It was the sound of the natural progression funk would've taken if it weren't interrupted by disco. I was completely hypnotized by the show's futuristic vision.

Hip-Hop as It Happened

Hip-hop busted down the door with guns blazing. The *Soul Train* timeline for artists' first performances goes like this.

1980, Episode 336, Kurtis Blow—This was the official flag planting for hip-hop's arrival, and Kurtis did it without lip-syncing "The Breaks." The audience's highly enthusiastic response to the performance was similar to the effect of Kool & the Gang's "Jungle Boogie" in 1974. Watching, you just knew that this sound was the sound of a new generation.

1981, Episode 361, Sugarhill Gang—Many may debate whether the Sugarhill Gang was authentic hip-hop or was put together in a contrived way for the branding of Sylvia Robinson's new label, Sugar Hill Records. Nonetheless, "Rapper's Delight" goes down in history. The great novelty was in performing the song without singing a note, like jazz-scatting onomatopoeias that fill in for words where a narrative doesn't exist.

1981, Episode 374, Frankie Smith—You have to give it to Frankie. For a guy with a generic last name, he sure did know how to spin the English language by fusing a nonsensical breed of slang into his music. Before Snoop Dogg put a "shizzle in his nizzle," there was a *plizace* for "Double Dutch Bus."

1983, Episode 414, Grandmaster Flash & the Furious Five—If history were to right its wrongs, I believe that Grandmaster Flash & the Furious Five would have been the featured act and not the support act for Evelyn King. Not to say that she was anything to sneeze at, with a platinum album, *Get Loose*, in her hands. But this was one of the few times the production crew made a wrong call and the revolutionary and more important artist was a side act. I am certain that in Don's eyes, since Evelyn had been around since 1977, he perceived her as more ubiquitous. Grandmaster was on an independent label, and the radio was very resistant, even though he did get some radio play. Still, Grandmaster's song "The Message" is very valuable—"life's a jungle, so watch your back."

1984, Episode 445, Newcleus—This Brooklyn-based b-boy crew was hip-hop's answer to Alvin and the Chipmunks with "Jam On It." They had a unique performance because the chipmunk-voiced break-dancers actually used the entire floor of the *Soul Train* set to perform, clearing the dancers out of the way and giving them more space to display their breaking skills, which instantly caught America's attention.

BELOW The Sugarhill Gang in Episode 361 on May 16, 1981.

HIP-HOP'S FIRST RECORD, *KING TIM III*, WAS FROM THE SOUL GROUP FATBACK BAND, AND OF COURSE DON'S GOOD FRIEND SYLVIA ROBINSON DECIDED TO PURSUE HER SON'S ENTHUSIASM FOR THIS NEW MUSIC COMING FROM THE BRONX. SO TECHNICALLY *RAPPER'S DELIGHT* IS THE SECOND HIP-HOP RECORD, RELEASED JUST A FEW MONTHS AFTER THIS ALBUM FROM FATBACK BAND.

ABOVE Frankie Smith goes to Hollywood on November 7, 1981. **BELOW** Newcleus put on a show that set the mood for '80s hip-hop.

IT'S WHO YA KNOW

Many of *Soul Train*'s game-changing hip-hop performances were made possible because of Don's relationship with Sylvia Robinson (of the duet Mickey & Sylvia), recording-artist-turned-record-executive and founder of Sugar Hill Records. This relationship between Don and an indie label is a great example of how networks and contacts were crucial to the show's success.

Further, nepotism ran deep when Don jazzed up the '80s. In Episode 343 on November 15, 1980, a notable jazz figure from the school of Miles Davis, percussionist James Mtume, visited the show. James was the son of American jazz saxophonist Jimmy Heath. Miles's fusion of rock and soul into his jazz was the inspiration that his backup musicians needed once they all went solo, and that included James.

In addition to Leon Sylvers, two other members of the Mtume group, guitarist Reggie Lucas and keyboardist Hubert Eaves III, were also record producers. Aside from Leon, all the people on stage (having come from jazz backgrounds) set the memes for soul music moving forward. Hubert would later leave the group to start another influential *Soul Train* favorite—D-Train. And Reggie's protégé was a girl from Detroit named Madonna. He produced her first record. Next to Leon, James Mtume kind of ran the charts in the first three years of the '80s with Stephanie Mills, Roberta Flack, and Roy Ayers, and for himself, with "Juicy Fruit," which was a massive hit in 1983. They all graced the *Soul Train* stage.

OPPOSITE TOP D-Train in Episode 390 on May 15, 1982. **OPPOSITE MIDDLE** Cameo in Episode 395 on June 19, 1982. **OPPOSITE BOTTOM LEFT** Sylvia Robinson performed with the Moments in Episode 98 on May 11, 1974. **OPPOSITE BOTTOM RIGHT** Sylvia Robinson with the Moments. **TOP** Cameo in 1985. **BOTTOM LEFT** Sylvia Robinson. **BOTTOM RIGHT** The System in Episode 533 on April 18, 1987.

1984, Episode 449, Run-D.M.C.—Run-D.M.C. marks the third phase of hip-hop culture, in that their presentation was accessible. They dressed like the people in your neighborhood—black hat, sneakers, sans spike accessories and feathers and boots and multicolors. Run's brother, Russell, was their manager and promoter, and his vision for the rap group was no flash and bare bones. You could say that the group was a precursor to Nirvana as far as their display of the "common man" superstars. They looked like the guys on the basketball court or rapping in the lunchroom.

1985, Episode 464, Fat Boys—Hip-hop was beginning its next lease on life and was being consumed by the public in massive quantities. Don actually seemed to genuinely like the Fat Boys, who endeared themselves to the host. Few rap groups didn't possess a hard machismo posture, but here were the non-threatening Fat Boys. For Don, seeing their humor and display of genuine kinship was a turning point. Of course, the novelty of beat boxing stirred instant excitement, especially when the trio broke out into an impromptu a cappella performance. The group recognized they had one chance to impress Don. They took it—and they nailed it.

1985, Episode 465, Whodini—Whodini's music cast a wide net, which caught the approval of the brothers on the avenue, as well as the professionals on the boulevard. I refer to them as the first adult contemporary hip-hop group, because they appealed to the twenty-three to thirty-two-year-old set. It wasn't midlife crisis hip-hop; it was classier and more mature. Their performance was less "street" oriented and more professional office water-cooler friendly—the kind of rap group your older brother in college was into. Russell Simmons once described them as "the S.O.S band who knew how to rap." The formula worked because their music was irresistible.

1985, Episode 488, UTFO—A byproduct of the new jack swing precursor, Full Force, UTFO didn't perform the song they became world famous for, "Roxanne, Roxanne." Instead they chose "Bite It," and their one ballad, "Fairy Tale Lover," which credits them with having been the first rap group to have a ballad on its album. But because they sang it and did not rhyme it, like LL Cool J did with "I Need Love," they often get overlooked when history gets rewritten.

1985, Episode 493, Doug E. Fresh—Don kept his feet firmly planted in the future with the booking of Doug E. Fresh. Don liked to blend his presentations of well-proven and riskier acts, but this is a rare episode in which all three acts were daringly assigned to the future. (The Jets and the Thompson Twins shared this episode.)

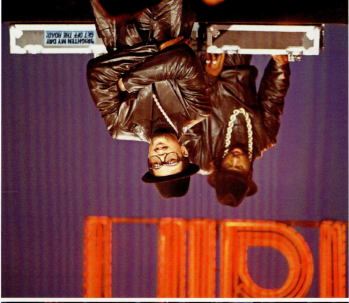

OPPOSITE TOP Grandmaster Flash & the Furious Five. **OPPOSITE MIDDLE UPPER** Run-D.M.C. **OPPOSITE MIDDLE LOWER** Don's endearing expression revealed that he gave props where props were due to the Fat Boys. **OPPOSITE BOTTOM** Whodini. **ABOVE** Slick Rick, Doug E. Fresh, and Barry B. in Episode 493 on December 14, 1985. **ABOVE RIGHT** None of us could live without our radios, thanks to LL Cool J.

1985, Episode 497, LL Cool J—LL started a shift in hip-hop, because he was one of the first to incorporate a pop song structure into his records. Before LL, hip-hop was an all-disco format; record labels were thinking in terms of seven-minute to fifteen-minute songs. The longer the record, the more frequently it played at clubs and discos. LL's vision for his music was to fit the radio format. Thus his songs lasted, on average, three minutes and thirty seconds, with sixteen-bar verse structures, followed by a chorus, then verse, chorus, verse, chorus. He ditched the endless showcase that hip-hop previously displayed and ended up on top.

1987, Episode 527, Beastie Boys—Personally, I think Russell Simmons' approach to marketing the Beastie Boys on his Def Jam label was a sly one. He knew that if he could apply the Colonel Tom Parker scenario, it would mean a marvelous payday for the Def Jam empire. Colonel Tom Parker once said that if he could find a white male singer that sang as well as his black peers, he would make a billion dollars. The person he found to be that gold mine was Elvis Presley. Russell thought that if he, too, could find his white Run-D.M.C., he would swim in cash. He broke into a chapter of hip-hop history slowly and steadily by first hiding an artist's identity. Just as Berry Gordy told the Isley Brothers they would not be on the cover of their album for "This Old Heart of Mine," because two white teens embracing on a beach would sell the music to a wider audience, Russell applied this rule to

REVOLUTIONARY HIP-HOP

The first three years of hip-hop and the commercial marketplace for it were seen as a post-disco party, and the two songs that Grandmaster Flash and the Furious Five performed on the show—"The Message" and "The Message II: Survival"—set the precedent for social commentary on hip-hop. When I first heard "The Message," it was probably equivalent to how John Lennon's "Imagine" affected a generation. The song described in detail the trash-filled conditions of the ghetto, and no matter where you were, you were put right there and could smell the piss in the train station and feel the broken glass cutting your feet. Grandmaster Flash and the Furious Five brought this realism to *Soul Train*.

Their performance took it to a new level, too. Grandmaster had grown up with groups like the Moments, the Originals, and Blue Magic, who were inspired by Motown. So even though Grandmaster Flash and the Furious Five was definitely a six-man hip-hop group, it still delivered its stuff with five-man group essence. And they took their choreography one step further by acting out the lyrics—staging fights and emitting tension with weapons and bats and chains. It was theater, too.

THE IDEA

the Beastie Boys. When I watched this episode, it was the first moment that I realized that my favorite Puerto Rican trio in hip-hop was not at all Puerto Rican. The only people who knew the Beastie Boys were white were the audiences Russell allowed them to play live for when opening for Madonna's Virgin Tour of 1985, where there wasn't a hip-hop fan to be found. That was their biggest widespread promotion, but because it wasn't for the hard-core hip-hop audience, they didn't risk blowing their cover. After, the Beastie Boys were hidden until their core fan base found them. Most of us in America, aside from native New Yorkers, had no idea that they were white—until this episode.

I found it surprising that as the first white rap artists to appear on *Soul Train*, they did not perform any of their singles, despite this being the same year that their monumental "Fight for Your Right" single hit the top of the charts.

I've been accused of not being up on hip-hop or not being a fan of hip-hop, which was never true. If you had a following and you were charting in the major industry magazines **Billboard***, and before that* **Cash Box***, we had a commitment that* **Soul Train** *was yours.*

—Don Cornelius

1987, Episode 553, Eric B. & Rakim—They represented the fourth generation of hip-hop, otherwise known as the "classic renaissance period." And everyone who name-checks *Soul Train* inside their rhyme, as Rakim did in "I Know You Got Soul," gets instant approval from the *Soul Train* audience.

1987, Episode 554, Public Enemy—After Grandmaster Flash's infusion of hard-hitting socially conscious lyrics into hip-hop came the most revolutionary hip-hop act hailing from, of all places, Long Island (!). They made Don's initial Afrocentric self awareness presentation hip again, thrilling adults and teenagers and all stops in between. My favorite Don reaction is in this episode. I use his line to this day when I watch an act take my breath away for the first time. "Wow . . . that was *frightening*."

1988, Episode 559, Kool Moe Dee—A rare example of a successful pioneer who easily changed with the times was former Treacherous Three member, Kool Moe Dee, who performed his title track "How Ya Like Me Now" from his platinum album.

1988, Episode 560, Heavy D & the Boyz—Always a fan favorite, the audience would often go wild during their performances. I always considered Heavy D & the Boyz adult contemporary hip-hop, a sucessor of Whodini.

OPPOSITE TOP The Beastie Boys had a meeting of the minds with Don in Episode 527. **OPPOSITE BOTTOM** Erik B. and Rakim. **TOP** Public Enemy gave a new flav to hip-hop in Episode 554. **ABOVE** Kool Moe Dee. **RIGHT** MC Hammer.

THE IDEA

1988, Episode 562, Salt-N-Pepa—One of the first all-female rap groups, this trio was hot, cool, and vicious as they promoted their second album, *A Salt with a Deadly Pepa*. Deadly they were, standing righteous and fearless in a male-dominated rap industry, setting the precedent for the female hip-hop artists to come in the '90s. They performed their insanely popular hit, "Push It," one of hip-hop's first platinum singles, which was met with enthusiastic response by the *Soul Train* Dancers.

1988, Episode 565, Dana Dane—Picking up where he and his former Kangol Crew partner Slick Rick left off, Dana brought his witty English accent, which he miraculously acquired growing up in Fort Greene, Brooklyn, to the *Train*. He did "Cinderfella Dana Dane," which was a Cinderella narrative told from Dana's point of view—a guy who wants to go clubbing but his stepbrother won't let him, until his fairy godfather comes to save him.

OPPOSITE TOP The First Ladies of Rap, Salt-N-Pepa. **OPPOSITE BOTTOM** EPMD. **ABOVE** Dana Dane. **TOP RIGHT** Rob Base & DJ E-Z Rock. **MIDDLE** Heavy D. **BOTTOM** MC Hammer in Episode 605.

1988, Episode 585, EPMD—Easily embraced, the members of EPMD were the first New York rappers to ditch the aggressive maniacal act and perform in a way that would be embraced by other regions of the country. Their pioneering "slow flow" style was more at home with fans from down south and the West Coast. They weren't wordy or nerdy when performing "Strictly Business" on *Soul Train,* but more California laid-back.

1989, Episode 597, Rob Base & DJ E-Z Rock—The hip-hop duo from Harlem rang in the omnipotent anthem of every bar across the Jersey Shore: "It Takes Two."

1989, Episode 598, Tone Lōc—A hip-hop phenomenon using a DIY approach to making his song and video (grand total $400 production budget), Tone created one of the first multi-platinum-selling singles in hip-hop history. His arrival on *Soul Train* couldn't have happened at a better time, as this year was the pinnacle of his career.

1989, Episode, 605, MC Hammer—It is quite fitting that the last hip-hop artist to appear on *Soul Train* in the '80s was MC Hammer. The James Brown of the hip-hop generation, who used street dancing and overall rapping and fashion presentation, was rap's greatest showman.

THE IDEA | **145**

THE ACTS

Just as my aunts, uncles, and parents cut their teeth on the moves showcased in the *Soul Train* Line of the '70s, my younger cousins and I learned break dancing from watching the show in the '80s. In 1983, in fact, between episodes 428 and 450, a slew of dancers joined the program. The torch was being passed. *Soul Train* had found a way to attract a new generation. America's first collective look at b-boy culture came that year, when Don showed the video for "Save the Overtime (for Me)," a new song by the first artists ever to appear on *Soul Train*, Gladys Knight & the Pips. The video had Gladys and it had the Pips, and I will now, as an older man, admit that when Don introduced the video, my twelve-year-old self saw this as a chance to take a four-minute break and grab another bowl of Captain Crunch. The maniacal cries of my cousin Marquis had me rushing back to the TV before I could even reach

We got another sound comin' out of Philly that's a sho' nough dilly.

—Don Cornelius

the kitchen. "They're spinning on their heads," Marquis cried. "The Pips are spinning on their heads."

He was exaggerating, of course. He had to be. I mean what human being in their right mind would ever believe that . . . OH MY GOD! . . . there they were, just like Marquis said. It wasn't the actual Pips, of course—they were b-boys on the street— but how was I supposed to explain to myself, or anyone else, that I had just seen a human being rotate with the quickness and agility of a figure skater or Michael Jackson, but not on their feet? They were on their backs, their shoulders, knuckles, and, yes, even their heads.

I had no clue what just hit me. But I missed the entire rest of the episode after running outside my grandmother's house to tell all of my friends what I just saw. I was known to be the neighborhood exaggerator, so no one believed that this was physically possible. Most dismissed it as a tall tale. I was the little boy who cried "break."

The Boys Are Back in Town

The new attitude of *Soul Train* had turned b-boy centric, and Don did a great job of seamlessly rolling into the '80s, offering something for everyone. But people who had traditionally been watching *Soul Train* every Saturday, like my aunts, started losing their connection with the show and weren't getting on board as much anymore. The first episode of Season 14, number 451, on September, 22, 1984, is the most b-boy friendly of the entire run, as all three artists—O'Bryan, New Edition, and Ollie & Jerry—demonstrated break dance's cousin pop locking.

This episode, O'Bryan's sixth appearance on the program, encapsulated the break dance culture. Right about then, everyone wanted to cash in on breaking fever, and in a genius attempt at hitting the lottery, he performed the break dancing anthem he had created, "Breakin' Together."

Ollie & Jerry's performance was also triumphant. Former LA studio musicians and disciples of Stevie Wonder and Ray Parker Jr. respectively, they performed the other break dancing anthem, "There's No Stopping Us," from the movie *Breakin'*. Incorporating outside dancers to hammer the point home, it was the beginning of having outside dancers and choreography augment performances on *Soul Train*. Dancers were suddenly the new "band." All you needed was a drummer, a singer, and a few break-dancers, and even the old guys looked hip.

Which brings us to New Edition. This is songwriter and producer Maurice Starr testing the waters. Maurice was the

PAGE 146 Parliament Funkadelic in Episode 362 on May 23, 1981. **OPPOSITE TOP LEFT** Luther Vandross has the floor to himself in Episode 520 on November 22, 1986. **OPPOSITE TOP RIGHT** The Before: Planet Patrol takes the stage in Episode 425 on October 29, 1983. **LEFT** The After: A whole new costume just a moment later in Planet Patrol's performance in Episode 425.

THE ACTS | **149**

first superproducer of the '80s and could see that the future of black music was paved with hip-hop. He attempted to knock the ball out of the park three times, first with Planet Patrol (Episode 425). "Play at Your Own Risk" marked the first time that an R&B group took a familiar song ("Planet Rock" by Afrika Bambaataa & the Soulsonic Force) and added lyrics to it. Their presentation was all about the costumes being outlandish, about the idea that the theater of it all was just as important as the music itself. That would also hold true with Starr's next grand slam, New Edition.

The question he set out to answer was if he, amidst all of the hip-hop hoopla, could make something old—the Motown-style five-man lineup—feel new. Or the better question: Could something new feel old?

NEW EDITION

In the '80s, the passing of the torch to the kids had begun. The older generation was feeling somewhat slighted and New Edition had to play both sides of the fence. Could they sell records to the new generation while still gaining the respect of their parents? Would a person like my father stand for a bunch of adolescent kids from Boston who wanted to add a little Run-D.M.C. to their Temptations?

This was the big feat for Maurice when he put together New Edition. He was selling Cholly Atkins meets Brooke Payne, incorporating b-boy culture with Motown traditional performance. It was a tall order to fullfill in their debut appearance in Episode 436, with Ray Parker Jr. headlining, on February 11, 1984. Maurice released a disgruntled New Edition from their contract with Streetwise Records, and they were signed to MCA after a bidding war in 1985. Ray coproduced their second album, titled *New Edition,* with Michael Sembello. They came back somewhat polished but it completely turned around in **EPISODE 466 ON JANUARY, 26, 1985**.

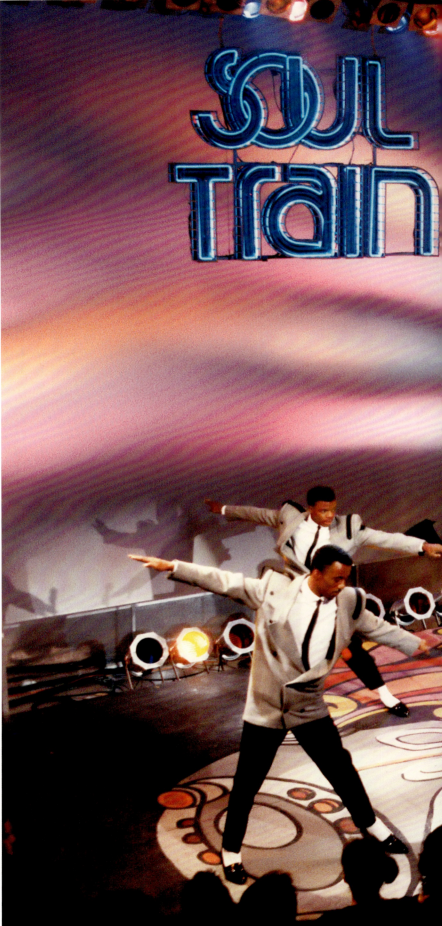

LEFT New Edition in the Johnny Gill years in Episode 574 on June 25, 1988. **ABOVE** New Edition in Episode 578.

THE ACTS | 151

New Edition came back as headliners this time. Here they really stepped into sophistication. They showed massive improvement in their presentation and successfully grabbed the torch formerly occupied by the Jackson 5. This third appearance continued their brand of b-boy-inspired moves, which told people like my father that they weren't trying to be the Temptations. They cleverly played it in the middle, infusing both the showman pizzazz of Cholly and the intricacies of a rock-steady dance crew like the New York City Breakers. The Temptations weren't about to do a human snake on the floor, but these guys could do Temptations moves. It was so well put together that even a traditionalist like my dad accepted it with a head nod.

New Edition's peak period could be attributed to the lasting power of their ability to read the times. To take the title from the Jackson 5 meant they had to sing well, entertain, and be influential in style, approach, music, and choreography. Truth be told—and I know this is blasphemous—but I would say that as a unit New Edition had the edge over the traditional Jackson 5. New Edition was a unit who had successful platinum success. But their biggest feat happened when they spawned off in multiple acts: solo careers for Bobby Brown and Ralph Tresvant, and the formation of new jack swing pioneers Bell Biv DeVoe by Ricky Bell, Michael Bivens, and Ronnie DeVoe. And while this was the last episode for Bobby Brown as a member of New Edition, the quartet came back the following season in Episode 489—to finish promoting their *All for Love* album.

Bobby Brown left his childhood friends from the Boston projects for a solo career in 1985. He was the third act of Episode 574 in 1988 with headliners . . . you guessed it, New Edition, who was at that time winning hearts with replacement member Johnny Gill. Bobby was, by then, a well-seasoned performer, and right into the early '90s, every little step he took was his prerogative.

RIGHT: New Edition in Episode 489 on November 16, 1985. **OPPOSITE TOP** Bobby Brown in Episode 574. **OPPOSITE BOTTOM** Johnny Gill.

EPISODE 499 AIRED ON APRIL 5, 1986. IN A RARE CANDID MOMENT, DON TURNED HIS ICONIC SIGN-OFF INTO AN APRIL FOOL'S DAY PRANK, SIGNING OFF INSTEAD WITH, "WISHING YOU LOVE, MONEY, AND POWER," TO WHICH THE AUDIENCE BOOED.

THE ACTS | 153

ABOVE On *Soul Train*, they certainly were the new kids on the block, but NKOTB was a crowd-pleaser in Episode 576, singing "Please Don't Go Girl." At the very least they asked politely.

THE FORCE M.D.'S

Like New Edition, the Force M.D.'s were also adored and respected by Don. This rap group from Staten Island was formed in the classic hip-hop tradition of Grandmaster Flash, the Treacherous Three, and Cold Crush Brothers (all members of the first wave of rap). Force M.D.'s calling card was the ability to harmonize—a requirement for a lot of first generation hip-hop groups. In fact, many of the pioneer hip-hop groups were influenced by the '70s groups—the Natural Four, the Impressions, and the Whispers. So if you had the dual ability to rhyme and harmonize, there was an instant advantage.

No group rode both sides of the wave better than the Force M.D.'s. When they signed to the Tommy Boy label in 1984, they were marketed as "Frankie Lymon meets the Cold Crush Brothers." They sang their Jam & Lewis produced "Tender Love." Interestingly, Jam and Lewis steered away from the patented Minneapolis funk formula, opting for Churban action.

NEW KIDS ON THE BLOCK

Having lost his chance at pay dirt with New Edition after they left his label for MCA, Maurice Starr came back to *Soul Train* with his revenge, New Kids on the Block. Don's cynical side, which questioned the staying power of the boy band movement, dominated the interview, just as his cynicism did in the Kurtis Blow interview of Episode 336 in 1980. I believe Don's attitude toward NKOTB was his way of showing loyalty to his five adopted "nephews" from Boston. However, just like his statement to Kurtis that hip-hop was a fad, Don's comment doubting that NKOTB would catch on was incorrect. After their appearance in Episode 576 on October 1, 1988, they became unstoppable.

A New Rubric

Season 12 kicked off on October 16, 1982, with the first of five very distinct episodes all on the same theme. In Episode 399, "Tribute to Joe Tex," the song that Barry White performed, called "Change," articulated the issues of Episodes 401–404, which acted like an instruction manual for how to deal with living in the '80s. This was intentional, as Don knew this was on the minds of soul music consumers. Thus it was no coincidence that Jermaine Jackson's futuristic new wave work with DEVO was showcased on Episode 401. This was followed by a booking of the BusBoys on Episode 402, a straight-up good-time rock 'n' roll band that toured with

ABOVE Morris Day in Episode 504 on May 10, 1986.
LEFT Don and Vanity 6.

Eddie Murphy after taking part in the soundtrack for *48 Hrs.*

In Episode 403 came Ozone, neither a rock band nor a new wave group but clearly futuristic. Protégés of Larry Blackmon of Cameo, Ozone was signed to Motown, and I imagine they likened themselves to a black version of DEVO—a black funk-punk hybrid. And in the last of the streak, Episode 404, Don gave Hall & Oates the lead position, which addressed what happens when you marry pop music with soul. It was an auspicious attempt to call out the elephant in the room—the fact that black music had indeed changed colors. The new color? Purple.

THE PRINCE REIGN

Episodes 408–410 alerted viewers that soul music would soon be an endangered species. The common denominator of all three of the featured acts on these episodes—Janet Jackson, the Time, and Vanity 6—was that each artist had directly and indirectly been filtered by Prince. Even though he did not perform on the show during the '80s, his greatest decade, he greatly influenced *Soul Train*. For instance, around 1982–1983, *Soul Train* stopped promoting Afro Sheen and started advertising Gentle Treatment. What does that have to do with Prince? He had since lost his Afro for a new wave curl at the top of the decade.

This was a period of irony in which having an Afro was no longer seen as having a sense of pride and the choice of style was to activate and curl. So Prince's reinforcement of this ideology—having an ambiguous racial identity and having "wet" hair—while radically

THE ACTS | **155**

ABOVE Vanity in Episode 452 on September 29, 1984.

pressing all the sexual taboo buttons that nobody wanted to touch numbed the Afrocentricity and pride accomplished the decade before. Prince was too busy unlocking the chambers of people's dirty souls to spend time worrying about how African we felt. He was endlessly talented like Stevie Wonder, as magnetic as James Brown, as young and attractive to girls as Michael Jackson, and so he played that sexual ambiguity to the hilt. A triple-threat with massive influence, Prince fueled music and culture directly and indirectly for the next twelve years.

JIMMY JAM AND TERRY LEWIS

In Episode 457 on November 3, 1984, Cherrelle made her debut. She was a protégé of Jimmy Jam and Terry Lewis formally of the Time. By the time Cherrelle returned with another Jam-Lewis associate, Alexander O'Neal, the following season in Episode 502, traditional soul music felt like it was six feet under. However, the powerhouse production team Jam and Lewis would hold a monopoly on black radio. By this time former boss Prince was trying to capitalize on a budding movie career, not to mention expand his musical horizons and find himself, and as a result his initial fan base felt like he was leaving his funk behind.

Jam and Lewis filled the funk base vacated by Prince and slowly took over black music's kingdom. Jam and Lewis subsequently became the new establishment for the sound of music for the next twenty years, which wasn't bad for two guys fired by Prince for producing S.O.S. Band's "Just Be Good to Me" (incidentally performed on the show in Episode 426 on November 5, 1983). Success is the best revenge, even for Alexander O'Neal, who had originally been passed over by Prince for the lead singer position of the Time, choosing Morris Day instead, who Prince signed in 1981. Promoting Alexander was Jam and Lewis's way of paying it forward.

IN ADDITION TO JIMMY JAM AND TERRY LEWIS, JESSE JOHNSON PRODUCED SOME OF JANET JACKSON'S MUSIC.

ABOVE The Mary Jane Girls in Episode 475 on April 13, 1985.

JESSE JOHNSON'S REVUE

Another graduate from Minnesota Funk University, Jesse Johnson was the former guitarist for the Time. In Episode 473 on March 30, 1985, Jesse had the opportunity to show off his breed of the Minnesota sound, an endeavor he described as something not of a "breakup" with the Time, but an opportunity for all the Time members to spread their wings and take music where they wanted to take it individually.

Minnesota established itself in the '80s the same way that Detroit was the epicenter for soul music in the '60s and Ohio was the epicenter of funk in the '70s. Minnesota became the midwestern city through which the future of R&B and pop would be filtered.

REGAL RIVALRY

One of the biggest rivalries in black music involved Prince and Rick James. In 1979, Prince was David to Rick's Goliath, and Rick had been publicly saying that Prince stole his funky utopian output, his multicultural and sexual presentation, and literally his girl (legend has it that initially Vanity was Rick's date at the American Music Awards). Thus began a decade of trash talk, mostly from Rick.

THE ACTS

THE PRINCE EPISODE WITHOUT PRINCE

Prince protégé acts were created because Prince was a multifaceted artist who needed side projects—like a creative schizophrenic. The Time was his street player side; Sheila E, was the credible band musician in him; Vanity/Apollonia 6, represented his feminine side. Prince used himself as a means to capture the pop world and all its money and power, and he never mixed the four entities up. But with the Time breaking up, Prince needed a vehicle to get himself on *Soul Train*, without doing it personally. Episode 484 on October 12, 1985, was the best Prince episode that Prince never appeared on, because for the entire interview portion, Prince was the only person Don wanted to talk about with Sheila E. For more than half of the interview, Shelia E. had to navigate loaded questions like "Is Prince really as mysterious as he pretends to be?" She did her best to respond, "There's love between us. He's real shy."

"Why won't Prince do interviews?" Don asked her. "You tell him that if he ever comes on *Soul Train*, I'm going to interview him." Prince's elusiveness wasn't exclusive to Don. The same month of Episode 484's broadcast, Prince granted *Rolling Stone* a Q&A, his first interview in the five years since he'd become a megastar.

Protégé Power: Punk Funk vs Purple Rock

One year before Janet Jackson would see that Minnesota was the new epicenter for soul music and hook up with Jam and Lewis, Scotland's Sheena Easton gladly let Prince remake her image. She dropped the Scottish "niceties" and revamped her image into a sex kitten. 1985 was the breakout year for all female protégé acts in the Prince and Rick James camp. The hit singles for both Sheena and the Mary Jane Girls were overtly sexual and *Soul Train* embraced them, which showed how far *Soul Train*'s ideology changed. The conservative postgospel presentation was out the window, and songs like "Sugar Walls" and "In My House" were aired without a second thought. So having both acts in Episode 475 on April 13, 1985, was as close to a Rick James versus Prince show as you could ever get. Each performance got a rousing response, especially from the male portion of the audience.

Episode 487 on November 2, 1985, marked a period when Prince's protégés and influencers began to register above the radar. Bands of the early and mid-'80s, perhaps the most overt being Ready for the World—a six-man band from Flint, Michigan, whose biggest hit, shared the name of Prince's protege, "Oh Sheila." With instrumentation identical to Prince's, and the Minneapolis sound there was no escaping his purple eclipse.

Blue-Eyed Soul

It took a few decades but by the '80s it was acceptable to realize that there were white people with soul. Part of that epiphany was due to bands like the Doobie Brothers, whose keyboardist and lead singer, Michael McDonald, had one of those voices that could be at home in any genre. After he left the Doobie Brothers to go solo, Michael appeared on Episode 408 on December 18, 1982, and it was no longer shocking or new to see a white guy creating blue-eyed soul. He had a waiting audience for "I Keep Forgettin'," a song appropriate for soul and pop music stations the world over.

Michael brought with him some of the best handpicked session musicians of the day who were joining the "go-for-a-solo-career" bandwagon—Louis Johnson of the Brothers Johnson on bass, Greg Phillinganes on piano, and Jeff Porcaro on drums. Don was impressed with this choice of musicians, which I like to believe indicated to Michael: Even the brothers and sisters love you. If these musicians are playing with you, you must be great.

Similarly, if you were white and on the Motown label, like Sam Harris, you were golden. Sam's initial celebrity came as a result of the first wave of *Star Search*. Before there was *American Idol*, Ed McMahon was Ryan Seacrest. Don had his hands in every musical outlet to make sure *Soul Train* was still the big shot in town. When

OPPOSITE Sheena Easton in Episode 584 on November 26, 1988.
LEFT Michael McDonald in Episode 408 on December 18, 1982.
BELOW Hall & Oates.

ABOVE Robert Palmer in Episode 603 on June 3, 1989. **RIGHT** Don Henley singing "All She Wants to Do Is Dance." **OPPOSITE LEFT** Whitney did not get emotional; she made it clear that Clive and she were going places. **OPPOSITE TOP** Michael McDonald high on life without the Doobies in Episode 408 on December 18, 1982. **OPPOSITE RIGHT** Culture Club arrives in Episode 502 on April 26, 1986.

Don booked Sam, he was already famous, and I believe that Don was trying to channel all of the *Star Search* talent of the time onto his show. Don's keeping his eye on televised competition like *Star Search* (which later turned out Justin Timberlake, Britney Spears, Dave Chappelle, Adam Sandler, Usher, Aaliyah, Sharon Stone, Christina Aguilera, Beyoncé, and many others) was another move you couldn't learn at Harvard Business School: zeroing in on talent that was filtering through a different system.

There was also another scouting system that Don didn't need to fight for. And that was the one run by Clive Davis at Arista Records. Even I knew back then of his power, and when Whitney Houston debuted in Episode 476 on April 20, 1985, even the village idiot knew she was going to be a household name at any given moment. Whitney wasn't the headline, though, because Don Henley was, and I clearly understood why. I was actually shocked that Don Cornelius was so knowledgeable about the Eagles' track record. He clearly acknowledged Henley's pedigree when he admitted, "I didn't know you had *that much* funk in you."

During the interview the Dons spoke about the history of the Eagles and Henley's shift to solo artistry. Don gave the viewing audience a lot of credit in his assumption that it was up to speed on Henley's rock history, which indicated to me that Don wasn't catering to his early demographic. The tone of the interview was presumptuous, as in *you already know this guy*, and that was probably because MTV was pervasive by this point.

And true to form of all of the "blue-eyed" soulers who visited the show, Henley came equipped with some of the best session musicians that lip-syncing can buy, making an impression that the band leader was "down."

Stature and status now meant everything to the *Soul Train* audience, so as long as you were the A-list elite, and the song could be danced to, you had an instant formula for winning. Henley's "All She Wants to Do Is Dance" encompassed the ingredients necessary to be a fan favorite.

160 | SOUL TRAIN

Expanding Horizons

When Spandau Ballet performed in Episode 478 on June 1, 1985, they were beside themselves, over-the-top in their enthusiasm for being on *Soul Train*. Their massive hit "True" was a ballad, but it was a ballad that didn't turn people off or seem cheesy. This was a booking that showed Don going for the gold, as Spandau Ballet's performance was simultaneous with their number one position on the charts.

However, the highlight of this episode was not Spandau Ballet, but a preview of *620 Soul Train*, the UK version of *Soul Train*, hosted by Jeffrey Daniel, formerly of Shalamar. Don was expanding the brand, which was a big deal pre-Internet—it was real news to me that people all over the world liked soul music. That was the most amazing thing to me about this whole episode. Instead of showing the band's music video at the midpoint of the show, Don made the declaration, "We are expanding our horizons, and I am proud to say that we started a completely different show."

I tend to think he would have wanted to syndicate the show, but instead they did an entirely different version with Jeffrey doing a very strange London accent. But he seemed primed for the position because Shalamar had actually been bigger in the UK than in the States. The show was called *620 Soul Train* and only lasted two seasons.

Even though it might have seemed random to some, there was always a method to Don's madness—a backstory and a formidable relationship—when it came to booking pop acts. Every booking had a common denominator, and what this one came down to was *book the hot act*.

"Take On Me" was climbing up the charts, and Don caught A-ha on the rise. In 1985–1986, the perceived notion on the part of chart-topping performers was, "I am too big for *Soul Train*," which is why you didn't see folks like Lionel Richie, Eddie Murphy, and Stevie Wonder on, despite all three holding top ten positions on the *Billboard* chart during that time. So for Don, it was a throwback to the days of needing a big act to book more celebrities. This became more ingrained in his mind in the early to mid-'80s, because even the African American celebrities were inaccessible to him, choosing touring, MTV, BET, and prime-time outlets to self-promote. This was a different tone than the one set in the '70s, when an established star like Michael Jackson

OPPOSITE LEFT Thomas Dolby in Episode 575 on September 24, 1988. **ABOVE** The Pet Shop Boys.

would still come on; back then, there was a feeling of loyalty and appreciation. But in the '80s, the overall mentality was "greed is good," so people weren't paying it forward anymore. Don, however, was too wise and too shrewd to let all of this get him down, so what filled the void was his ability to get top foreign acts to have the "honor" of appearing on the show.

If you took away the MTV-friendly UK acts that appeared on *Soul Train* during Season 15, you would have half a season. What made the season notable was not only that it embraced acts of other genres, but that Don got lucky in that these acts were eventually hit makers. I was excited to see the Pet Shop Boys in Episode 506 on May 24, 1986, because they had their new hit out, "West End Girls." And airing up-and-coming stars is what had made *Soul Train* cutting edge.

But Don couldn't last on too many Temptations or Four Tops appearances, no matter how loyal he was to their brands. Hip-hop and the UK's electronic movement kept *Soul Train* alive. From Season 15 on, the only truly gargantuan platinum-selling black artists who came on the show were Cameo and New Edition. Which is why A-ha was a coup; they were a band that would have a monster hit. Seasons 14 and 15 would be the highest Nielsen-rated in the history of *Soul Train*.

THE ACTS

THE MOVES

By 1980, one of the most coveted gigs in America was being a regular dancer on *Soul Train*. What had been somewhat of a novelty in the 1970s began to draw people with a desire for fame. The days of kids gathering at Dinker Park were replaced with dance coordinators and scouts who headed out to LA clubs in search of college girls who had average moves in superior packages. The cast, which was once primarily African American was becoming mixed—the iconic Asian American dancer Cheryl Song joined up in 1976—as Don set out to embrace a broader audience.

SOUL TRAIN

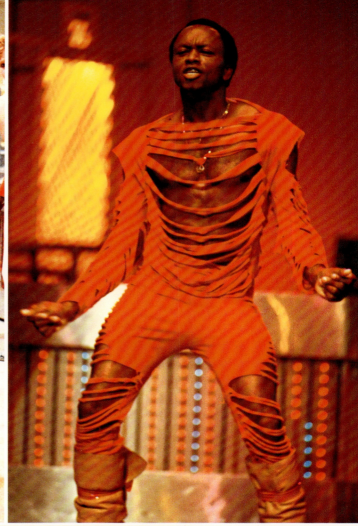

PAGE 164 Nothing says "Welcome to the '80s" like a pair of leg warmers. **PAGE 166 TOP** B-boy culture has a double meaning with this unique dance move. **PAGE 166 BOTTOM LEFT AND MIDDLE** Don't try this headspin at home, though we often did outside our house in Philly. We didn't have the handy helmet though. **PAGE 166 BOTTOM RIGHT** The enthusiasm of the audience was always infectious. **PAGE 167** I don't recall this period being as cheesy as this, but it was fun nonetheless. **OPPOSITE** Dancers welcomed one of their own when Jody Watley headlined in Episode 543 on September 19, 1987. **ABOVE LEFT** The stunts just kept on coming with these dancers in fat suits eating Kentucky Fried Chicken. **ABOVE RIGHT** One of Reggie Thornton's many, many, many crazy outfits. **RIGHT** Fashion became flashier as dancers vied for camera time.

As the dancers lined up behind the studio gates, the competition to get in was fierce. Even though certain dancers might have been "invited" by a producer or scout, they still had to fight their way in. And what they were fighting for was a chance to change their lives. I call it the Shalamar Effect, after the group launched from a trio of *Soul Train* dancers, most notably Jeffrey Daniel and Jody Watley. They weren't alone—many *Soul Train* dancers of the '70s went on to enjoy successful careers as singers, choreographers, and actors, thanks to the opportunities their exposure on the show afforded them. So it was only natural that this new generation of kids would have one thing in mind: camera time.

Yes, there were dancers who didn't hope to achieve supercelebrity, like Rosie Perez, but generally there was a notable shift in the new school of dancers. Their role became less about creating trends

ABOVE LEFT A Medley of Masks, the costumes became synonymous with Odis Medley's style. It was the only way to upstage Louie Carr (right). **ABOVE RIGHT** Just when you thought he couldn't get any more outrageous, Odis would surprise you with an outlandish idea. **OPPOSITE** No longer eager kids from the local schools, the dancers in the '80s came to show their professional dance training, like Aretha Jackson, who could high kick like no other.

and wowing the audience with inventive dance moves, and more about developing unique personas in order to brand themselves.

In my opinion, the '80s saw much less original dancing and more things that were easier to swallow—music included. Famous dancer and choreographer Lester Wilson created a dance called the Soul Train for the show, which the dancers ended up only doing for half of 1980. An organized dance took away from individual dancers' ability to set themselves apart, be noticed, and get discovered. The show's focus was migrating; Don stopped doing the dance spotlights, which meant nobody was being showcased anymore. The Soul Train History Book segment, in which Don aired clips of previous episodes, replaced it, followed by music videos, which made the Soul Train Line even more critical for catching airtime.

Enter Louie Carr, who exuded arrogance and attitude, and mastered the art of dancing without ever dancing. He waved his finger, struck a pose, gave a snarly expression, and the next thing you know, a generation of non-dancers (like me) thought they could light up a dance floor. Then you had Odis Medley, who turned Saturday mornings into a hybrid of The Rocky Horror Picture Show and Disneyland as he dressed up in crazy masks and costumes. Where else could you see a dancing elephant, a Cyclops, or Bozo the Clown on a riser? These "characters" began to emerge instead of dancers: *the girl with the butt-length hair* (Cheryl Song), *the guy who dressed like a Bergdorf mannequin* (Marco DeSantiago), *the pie-in-the-face guy* (Tom Evans). Vying for camera time created another habit that Don was not fond of—dancers "fraternizing" with artists.

The status the dancers achieved on Soul Train trickled down to other people who wanted their own claims-to-fame, like young fashion designers who hung around outside the studio walls soliciting dancers to wear their designs on air. The era of dancers expressing themselves with homemade or personally embellished clothes had come to a close, and now dancers were hitting the stores on Melrose Avenue or working as live billboards. The result was a much more homogenized look.

> *A new groove that'll make you move real smooth.*
>
> —Don Cornelius

SOUL TRAIN

Meet the Cast

ROSIE PEREZ

I remember *Soul Train* becoming a problem in my house when Rosie Perez crawled across the floor in the Barry White/Shanice Wilson Episode 548 on October 24, 1987. And what made her even more smoking was that she was a college girl attending Los Angeles City College and studying biology. She was recruited for *Soul Train* after being discovered in a dance club.

Rosie's sexuality was a bit exploited on the show. She opened the *Soul Train* Line segment and was always encouraged to shake what her mama gave her. Other female dancers were also soon being exploited. But Don couldn't have it both ways. It wasn't fair to have Rosie dressing and dancing the part of video vixen and then be angry when male performers

LEFT Rosie Perez once joked that this was the only move she had.
BELOW A scene that stole the show and raised eyebrows with Don, Keith Sweat and Rosie Perez in Episode 548 on October 24, 1987.

ABOVE Cheryl Song. **RIGHT** Maybe Rosie wasn't lying when she said she only had one move, but she was still a fan favorite, as was Marco DeSantiago (left).

noticed. It is said that Rosie first got yelled at by Don when she supposedly got too close to Run-D.M.C. In self-defense she told Don she was talking to them because she and Darryl McDaniels went to the same high school back in Queens. Rosie was put on warning not to cross the line again or else she'd be kicked off the show.

By the time of the infamous Episode 561 on March 19, 1988, in which she danced suggestively with Keith Sweat during his performance, Don's patience had run out. Legend has it that Don excused Rosie from the show because of that scene, but in actuality Rosie had already begun her exodus as a sought after choreographer and actress. Stardom was around the corner.

CHERYL SONG

When Cheryl Song debuted in 1976, she was the first Asian dancer on the show, and she continued to dance her way across racial barriers on *Soul Train* until 1990. She became not only a *Soul Train* institution, but a visual darling whose long locks, numerous trips down the *Soul Train* Line, elaborate outfits, and dance styles earned her the status of *Soul Train* icon.

Cheryl attended the predominantly black Dorsey High School in Los Angeles. Many of her friends in school were on *Soul Train,* including Jeffrey Daniel and Jody Watley, so Cheryl was brought onto the show as a dare. It was like, *Let's see what the reaction will be when she comes onto the show.*

Cheryl loved to dance and craved a safe haven where she could express herself and find respite from a difficult childhood. She was immediately placed on the risers, which didn't fare well with some of the dancers. While Cheryl didn't go to the show in search of a career in show business, she couldn't help but be recognized. Eventually her connections to *Soul Train* led her to appear in Rick James's "Superfreak" video and Michael Jackson's "Beat It."

After she left the show, Don hired Cheryl as an instructor at his dance studio in West Hollywood. Later she worked in the production office for *Soul Train*.

MARCO DESANTIAGO

With a tenure only one year short of Cheryl Song's, Marco DeSantiago spent thirteen years on *Soul Train* (1977–1990). While he wasn't known for being the best dancer, he brought a sense of high fashion to the show. After the popularity of *Saturday Night Fever*, Marco started doing his hair just like crooner Barry Gibb's—blown back and feathered—which earned him the nickname "Black Barry Gibb."

Unless dancers came to the show with a partner, they were paired with another dancer. Marco was matched with Dina Rivera. He began his fashion forwardness by dyeing his clothes at the last minute in an attempt to coordinate with what Dina was wearing. His first rule was "find clothing that fits you and

THE MOVES

complement the partner." His second was to compensate for his mediocre dancing ability by infusing a lot of heart. When he danced with a girl, he danced with her like she was his whole world, and would look her in the eye. This earned him a reputation for being smooth.

Marco taught himself how to "Hollywood" his clothes without spending money, and he learned to dig for discounts and wait for sales. He aspired to have an international Euro flair, emulating what he saw in *GQ*. He liked suit jackets, but on his terms, and managed to find orange jackets and match them with lime green shirts and fluorescent ties. Whether he wore a sash around his waist or a belt outside his pant loops, Marco was too humble to consider himself a trendsetter, saying, "It was just my duty to do it for *Soul Train*."

CRYSTAL MCCAREY

Crystal McCarey's Chicago roots tied her to Don in more ways than location. "So you dance? Let's see what you can do," Don said to Crystal at her 1976 audition. She danced for most of "I Love Music" by the O'Jays, and after Crystal was congratulated for passing the test, she let Don know of their connection. He turned around slowly and said, "You are Barbara McCarey's daughter?"

Barbara McCarey had been one of the Moulin Rouge Hotel showgirls in the first fully integrated Las Vegas casino. Don remembered this about Crystal's mom when he met her at a press event in Chicago. He also said Barbara was one of the most beautiful women in Chicago.

Crystal came to the show the daughter of a dancer, but her intention was not to get a big break as a dancer, but to learn the behind-the-scenes of show business. "I was always impressed watching Don on the set and how he fine-tuned the show," she said. "When he would come down from makeup, he wanted to be sure the right dancers were selected for the stage and risers and would go over the run sheet of the music that would be played and the artists that were going to perform. It was all a process and I studied this process for all the thirteen years I was on the show and was able to take what I learned to become a community television producer."

Aside from making her production dreams come to fruition, Crystal is known for having had several different privileges with some of the most famous guests on the show. She danced onstage with Marvin Gaye during his last television appearance in 1983 and got to meet the Jackson 5 twice, once in Chicago and the other time on the show in 1979.

"Michael and Jermaine told me and Cheryl Song that we were their favorite *Soul Train* dancers at the time," said Crystal. And when Little Richard came to the show, he brought his piano, nicknamed "Ethel" after his aunt, and yelled out to Crystal in the audience to come up on the stage.

ABOVE LEFT Crystal McCarey. **ABOVE RIGHT** Cheryl Song and Derek "Foxtails" Fleming in 1984.

DEREK "FOXTAILS" FLEMING

In the 1980s and early '90s, "LL DFox" was always dressed to the nines in all of the latest fashions. Derek did the Scramble Board at least five times and famously got to ask a question to Diana Ross during her tribute show.

Derek got his nickname because he wore foxtails with most of his outfits, and others, such as Full Force and Grandmaster Flash, eventually caught on to the trend. Shabba Doo even sported a foxtail in the movie *Breakin'*, but Derek was the first to do it on *Soul Train*.

Because he was a *Soul Train* dancer, Derek got to do cameos with Thelma Houston, Sybil, Sister Sledge, Evelyn Champagne King, Carrie Lucas, and Little Richard when they came to the show. He also danced onstage with Sheila E., but the segment was reshot after he was told to come off the stage. The same thing happened when Janet Jackson came to the show. Don reprimanded Derek for going on the stage to dance with her, and her segment was reshot.

JULIETTE HAGERMAN

Juliette Hagerman began on the show in 1984. Her good friend from Chicago, Diana Hicks, who was already dancing on *Soul Train*, invited her to come to a taping. Juliette had an opportunity to work with singer Nona Hendryx the very first time she was on the show. Nona needed backup dancers during her performance, and Don picked Juliette and two other girls for this.

Juliette is most known for a twin sister act she did with Michelle Stevenson, another featured dancer on the show. One time Michelle said that people thought they looked like sisters, so a designer named Tony Briggz suggested they dress similarly. Then the directors started having them dancing together side by side, looking like twins. They sometimes even went down the

Soul Train Line together. To this day, people come up to Juliette and ask about her twin.

Soul Train gave Juliette the platform to do music videos, her first being Billy Ocean's "Suddenly." Her other credits include Stevie Wonder's "Go Home" and Midnight Star's "Operator."

Spotlight on Louie "Ski" Carr

Known for his "Cutty Finger Salute," only Louie Carr could wag his index finger in the air and then use it to reel in every woman from LA to Wichita to Buffalo. Like him or not, he goes down in history as the *coolest Soul Train* dancer of all time.

Louie began on the show in 1979 as a nondescript dancer on the floor. He was the tallest one in the crowd and and did more posing than dancing. He had style. Louie became better known as Lou Ski because he jumped from one riser to another, and his friends said he looked like a skier doing the move.

Even though Jermaine Stewart had the mid '70s Michael Jackson style going, Louie channeled his spirit from 1979 to 1985. From 1978 to 1982, you were lucky if you got to see Michael Jackson perform six times a year on television. It's not like his videos came on every day; you were basically starving for that magic. So in a time before YouTube and DVRs, Louie filled the void. He did all of Michael's signature moves and rock star poses. This is as close as I would get to Michael until my parents got MTV.

TOP LEFT Juliette Hagerman in a Toney Briggz design. **TOP RIGHT** Louie Carr and Sheila Lewis. **ABOVE** A product placement promotion for *Soul Train*–branded jackets, starring Louie Carr and Nieci Payne (left).

THE MOVES | 175

A Hip-Hop Skip and a Jump Down the *Soul Train* Line

The hip-hop generation was effectively the first generation to grow up with *Soul Train,* so the *Soul Train* Line was like the Holy Grail or something on a bucket list for hip-hoppers who came to perform on the show. While other artists on the show were part of the *Soul Train* legacy, members of the hip-hop generation were outsiders, and therefore even if they didn't know how to dance, they wanted to go down that Line. Louie Carr made dancing accessible to guys like the Fat Boys by giving them permission to simply pose their way down the Line. Other hip-hoppers who made it down the Line were Run-D.M.C. and Kid 'n Play.

BELOW Crystal Calhoun gives Kid 'n Play something to sing about. **OPPOSITE** Looking like a kid in a candy store, Darryl McDaniels makes his *Soul Train* Dance Line dream come true.

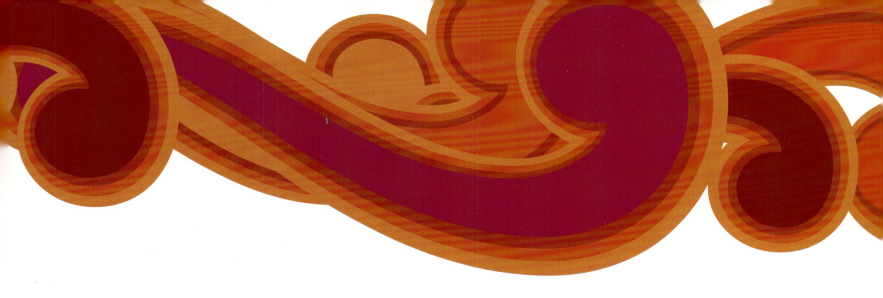

THE BIG MOMENTS

In the early days, the *Soul Train* interviews were smooth sailing, and Don was a confident captain. As the show went on, as the acts became more diverse, the interviews grew more unpredictable and more riveting. The homogenous brotherhood of a decade earlier gave way to interviews that could either throw Don for a loop or lead him to reminisce about the good old days. They could be inconsequential, or surreal, or surprisingly laced with gravitas. You just never knew.

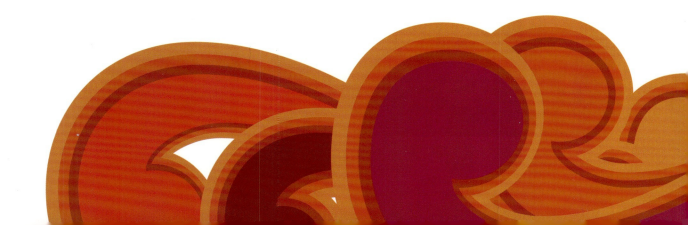

A Salute to Rick James

In 1981, Rick James had an album so big he had to go on the show twice to promote it. But before he was known for *Street Songs* (which featured the hits "Give It to Me Baby" and "Super Freak"), Rick's modest beginnings were a part of the *Soul Train* legacy.

In 1978 when the then thirty-year-old Rick appeared on Episode 276 with Jerry Butler, Rick was the supporting act and a normal new guy, so the experience was a humbling one for him. In Episode 308 on October 20, 1979, Rick brought with him his protégé Teena Marie, a five-feet-tall white girl who could match Aretha note for note. Along with the distraction of Don's interest in the novelty of Teena's soul pedigree, Rick wasn't the focal point of show.

By Episode 338 on October 11, 1980, the playful, crazy Rick started to surface. During this period, he put out his least-successful album, *Garden of Love,* a laid-back hippie pop record that was reminiscent of his Canadian rock-soul fusion band the Mynah Birds, whose lineup once included a young Neil Young. But fans wanted the funk. This marks the lone time that Rick was promoting music that wasn't nationally celebrated on the show. He returned to the show triumphant in Episode 365 but still not quite satisfied with the lack of royal treatment that he felt he deserved.

180   SOUL TRAIN

With his tail between his legs, he went back to his mother's home in Buffalo. There, the inspiration started coming to him and he wound up with *Street Songs*. It's an understatement to say that his star status grew to a dizzying height, with *Street Songs* going triple platinum and Rick selling out arenas four or five nights in a row; it was close to a miracle how fast his career turned around.

By Episode 371 on October 17, 1981, Rick was at the pinnacle of his career, and nothing said success better than Don giving Rick his own "Salute to" show. But the Rick who showed up had some sort of chip on his shoulder, and frankly, I was taken aback by the entire interview.

Rick gave it to Don: "Do you remember when you said I wouldn't make it?"

I was ten at the time, and I knew that this was tense and highly personal, as I didn't recall Don saying anything like that to Rick in previous episodes. Something was awkward, and it made me feel nervous and uncomfortable. Even now I still fast-forward through it because I am not used to seeing Don act so uncharacteristically. Until then no guest had had made Don lose his cool, but there's a first time for everything, and Rick holds the title. He broke every interview rule and basically railroaded the segment. Don tried to begin with his trademark introduction of the band, which meant that band members stated their own names. But Rick wasn't having it. Interrupting Don as he was about to prompt the first band member to introduce himself, Rick went around and pointed frantically to each member, shooting off their names, and packaging his backup girls as "the Mary Jane Girls."

Don's expression was of plain annoyance. But then, Rick ignored Don's interview questions, choosing instead to interact with the audience, which in turn meant that the audience was ignoring Don, too. Don tugged on Rick's arm and maneuvered him back into earshot. "I get the picture. Close your coat," he ordered Rick, as Rick continued to egg on catcalls from the audience, showing off his pink shirt beneath his white single-breasted sport jacket.

The whole thing looked like something Rick cooked up, dreamed about incessantly, and then played over and over in his head as vindictive payback. Or maybe I exaggerated the situation. Either way, I still don't like it.

PAGE 178 One of those interview moments when you wish you were in Don's head. **OPPOSITE LEFT** Teena Marie, certainly the queen of blue-eyed soul in Episode 571 on May 28, 1988. **OPPOSITE TOP** Rick James with his band. **TOP** Rick James in all his glory. **LEFT** Rick James with Val "Lady V" Young at backup (right). Val became famous after meeting Rick and being promoted by him as the "Black Marilyn Monroe."

THE BIG MOMENTS

LL Cool J

On March 22, 1986, eighteen-year-old LL Cool J walked on the *Soul Train* stage with an extremely enormous boom box and used it as a prop for his performance of "I Can't Live without My Radio." What makes Episode 497 all the more memorable is Louie Carr holding up a much smaller radio, which was passed around the audience. The crowd was hyped, singing along to the lyrics. It was like feeding rock candy to a three-year-old at bedtime; they were screaming, bouncing up and down, throwing things. No one could stop the adrenaline rush, even as Don emerged onstage for his interview portion. And so the fatherly Don scolded the audience: "Wait. Wait. That's enough, y'all."

You can see Don trying to grasp what this "scratching and catching" was all about. But his opposition to hip-hop still came through in statements like, "Tell us how you got started in this . . . *thing* you do" and, "Fascinating art, gentleman," which closed the interview. Don even put LL in his place when he interrupted Don's closing remarks. He turned to LL and said, "Hey, J, you did your thing, now let me do my spiel, okay, brother." It wasn't a question.

It was a power struggle between generations, with the kids staking claim to a music genre and culture that finally felt all their own and not their parents'. But Don gave a subtle reminder that he was still very much in charge.

TOP LL Cool J performed "I Need Love" and "I'm Bad" in Episode 552 on November 21, 1987. **ABOVE** LL with Don in Episode 552. **OPPOSITE TOP** Reverend Jesse Jackson with Don in Episode 396 on June 26, 1982. **OPPOSITE BOTTOM LEFT** Teddy Pendergrass in Episode 340 on October 25, 1980. **OPPOSITE BOTTOM RIGHT** The Yarbrough and Peoples puppet show . . . only on *Soul Train*.

Teddy Pendergrass

When Teddy Pendergrass came on the show at the absolute peak of his career on October 25, 1980, it would eerily be his last performance on the show before he was paralyzed. In hindsight, this makes the interview portion of Episode 340 one of the weightier ones. It was also atypical in that Don emulated a talk show format—two men in the studio talking—as opposed to engaging the audience.

Don dressed down and wore jeans, so you got the feeling it was "casual workday" at *Soul Train*. And they simply talked about the dark side of Teddy's success. I don't know how much anyone bought the claims that Teddy wasn't an alcoholic womanizer, but the conversation seemed genuine. There was no other outlet for him to be interviewed at length on a national level at the time, so here we saw an interview being used for much more than humanizing; it was for redemption. His hit tour "For Ladies Only" painted an oversexed image of him as an artist. Men were even banned from concerts.

But during the interview, Teddy told Don that in reality he was just a quiet boy from Pennsylvania, shy and humble. Two years after this taping, on March 18, 1982, the quiet country boy from Pennsylvania crashed his Rolls-Royce on the way home from a party.

Yarbrough & Peoples

In 1980, Yarbrough & Peoples had an insanely hot hit on their hands with "Don't Stop the Music." When I first heard that song with its helium-induced–sounding backup vocals, "You don't really want to stop," I couldn't help but envision a bunch of puppets singing the Greek-style chorus. So, when Yarbrough & Peoples performed on *Soul Train* in Episode 352 on March 14, 1981, with four sock puppets positioned on the risers, it went down in my book as "the cute episode" as well as the "I can't believe they actually did that episode." Only on *Soul Train* could it seem normal to have a bunch of puppets singing backup to a verse like "I just wanna rock you all night long."

THE BIG MOMENTS

ABOVE Patti LaBelle in Episode 375. **RIGHT** The new and improved Pointer Sisters.

The Pointer Sisters

Working since 1969, the Pointer Sisters were the one act with origins in the chitlin circuit who slowly became subculture darlings, and eventually achieved pop music pay dirt. It really started with Episode 353 on March 21, 1981, where the trio promoted their comeback hit "He's So Shy." They eschewed the cutesy Andrews Sisters costumers and the gimmicks and sang middle-of-the-road adult-oriented contemporary music.

But the Pointer Sisters weren't finished yet. Their appearance in Episode 442 on April 21, 1984, was the definite victory lap with "Jump," leading to the biggest pop success of their career—multiplatinum.

Patti LaBelle

EPISODE 375 ON NOVEMBER 14, 1981, marked the return of Patti LaBelle as she turned in her most inspired performance of her eight appearances on *Soul Train*, singing "Somewhere over the Rainbow." Usually when a song ended, the theme animation came on after about four seconds. But this performance sung live (Patti never ever lip-synced, even when she had backing tracks) moved the audience to the point where the applause went on through the showing of the animation. Nobody could affect an audience the way Patti could.

TOP 10 ALERT

THE BIG MOMENTS

ABOVE Jermaine Jackson and Don joking around in Episode 401 on October 30, 1982. **RIGHT** El DeBarge (center) returns as a force to be reckoned with, complete with backup dancers (pictured here) also in Episode 401. **OPPOSITE LEFT** Joining her brother Jermaine on the show, La Toya Jackson marks her spot on *Soul Train* in Episode 342. **OPPOSITE RIGHT** El DeBarge in Episode 591 on March 11, 1989.

A Salute to Jermaine Jackson

The bigger Michael Jackson got in the early '80s, the more Don cultivated an already strong relationship with Jermaine Jackson. Don had always been very good to Jermaine after the Jacksons disbanded, encouraging his talents and his endeavors during their interviews. Episode 401 on October 30, 1982, was a salute to Jermaine, in which his two sisters, La Toya and Rebbie, were his backup singers.

Jermaine also used this appearance as an opportunity to introduce his protégé DeBarge—a group morphed from my favorite band of the '80s (and Jermaine's other protégé), Switch. DeBarge was wet behind the ears; they hadn't gone through the Motown training school that Jermaine experienced, which was synonymous with having the best choreography around. As a result, DeBarge was notorious for zero coordination. I could tell that the music itself was their priority and not the presentation. Nonetheless, DeBarge became show favorites, making three appearances over the course of seven years. Bunny, El, and Chico, who was never part of the band, would all make solo performances within that time span, as well.

In the 1980–1982 season, artists were taking their leaps of faith into the pop world hoping for a big payoff, and Jermaine was no exception. Creatively he did a great job, as he left his comfort zone and collaborated with DEVO on "Let Me Tickle Your Fancy." The song stands the test of time; it still works, but it was never a massive hit. What added salt to the wound was that about a month and a half after the single's release, Jermaine's brother, Michael, collaborated with Eddie Van Halen, which resulted in "Beat It."

186 | SOUL TRAIN

EL DEBARGE BREAKS OUT

DeBarge's performance in Episode 431 on December 10, 1983, was one of those pet peeve moments for me, when the support act was actually as important as the headline act, which was officially Herbie Hancock. If I were to have called that tie-breaker, I would've given DeBarge the top spot. Why Don wasted two headliners in one show, I'll never know. It took the balance away from future guests. DeBarge could've definitely led this show, and as it stands, this should have been a victory lap for the group. This was one of DeBarge's most stellar performances—so stellar that Don refused to believe Eldridge DeBarge could sing in as high a register as he did unless he felt depressed or emotional. Don thought the only way to sing that high was if you were on the verge of tears. This led to Don getting El DeBarge to sing a cappella, launching him as a star. He became a force to be reckoned with after this performance.

THE BIG MOMENTS

OPPOSITE Marvin Gaye left it all on stage in his tribute show. **TOP LEFT** Cheryl Song gives movement to an already earth-rattling performance. **TOP RIGHT** A lasting image of song, dance, and class was Marvin's last gift to *Soul Train*. **ABOVE** The audience knew how lucky they were.

A Tribute to Marvin Gaye

By the 1980s, my elders had pretty much come to terms with the fact that *Soul Train* was now a show for the "kids." But one Saturday when my Aunt Sharon was getting her hair done upstairs at Grandma's house and they heard Sid McCoy's announcement of "A Tribute to Marvin Gaye," they got excited. I was highly disappointed that I needed to watch sixty minutes of boring Marvin Gaye. I mean, I thought "Sexual Healing" was okay, but it was no "Billie Jean." At the time, the only part of **EPISODE 417 ON JUNE 11, 1983**, that I thought was cool was the fact that Don let Marvin's then eight-year-old daughter, Nona, introduce her daddy.

I didn't understand that Marvin had gone through five years of hell, living in exile in Europe, sleeping in a bread truck in Hawaii, barely surviving as he lived the life of a gypsy and a rich homeless person (living in Belgium) before returning to America to make one of the biggest hits of his career. I did not appreciate what it must've taken Marvin to get back to this point, and to do it on *Soul Train*. And I would be haunted by my missing the point when on April 1, 1984, Marvin was killed by his own father.

Without a doubt, this program was one of the finest in *Soul Train*'s history. To top it off, Marvin's last song, " 'Til Tomorrow," was performed with seven signature *Soul Train* Dancers, including Cheryl Song, onstage and slow dragging with Marvin.

THE BIG MOMENTS | 189

ABOVE The always funny and very sly like a Redd Foxx.

Soul Train Spectrum

Episode 467 on February 2, 1985, was an experiment so over the top it worked. Ever the traditionalist, Don let a sixty-three-year-old Redd Foxx promote his new comedy record, *Live 85*, on *Soul Train*. As part of his act, Redd showed the kids how they "did it back in the day." And when Redd performed, he didn't just do comedy. He did jazz, hoofing with the Nicholas Brothers. Hoofing is the lost art of tap dancing, and Redd's range was too impressive for it to be seen as just "old people" stuff.

On *Soul Train* you got to see artists who were influential and had their heydays in the '50s and '60s, but rarely did you see an artist who was at the height of his power in the 1940s. Redd's nightclub act was really the precursor to Richard Pryor's, and Redd re-created this rich, vibrant atmosphere on the *Soul Train* stage.

The fact that Don would take a comedy icon like Redd and pair him on the same episode with a polar opposite like the R&B singer Rockwell wasn't by accident. Don was expanding his audience, always cognizant of MTV breathing down the neck of *Soul Train*. So, to keep the kids, as well as the Aunt Sharons of the world, happy, Don experimented with a balanced booking of traditional soul and "alternative" artists, i.e., hip-hop.

A great example of this was Episode 444 on May 5, 1984, when Dionne Warwick was paired with the New York City Breakers. I was thirteen, and this was one of the most exciting shows of the season because Don added a little spice that would've otherwise turned off a kid like me, and prevented it from becoming a boring traditionalist disaster.

The New York City Breakers were the dance troupe brainchild of Michael Holman—the downtown cultural leader and former art partner of Jean-Michel Basquiat. Episode 444 marked the first time break dancing was performed live on *Soul Train*. In some ways, this might have been an easier hip-hop pill for Don to swallow than the music itself because the art of breaking seemed like more of an entertaining challenge than the music. The b-boy culture wasn't yet validated as a true art form, but the dance aspect of the culture had the eyes and ears of naysayers open because they were simply mind-blown by what they saw.

Future episodes in which Don showcased the *Soul Train* spectrum included Berlin and the Controllers (Episode 460), the Temptations and the Fat Boys (Episode 464), the Four Tops and Spandau Ballet (Episode 478), Go West and Rosie Gaines (Episode 483), and Rick Dees and UTFO (Episode 488).

Herbie Hancock

In Episode 431 on December 10, 1983, Herbie Hancock came on *Soul Train* to impressively and historically perform "Rockit"—which is saying a lot since there is only so much you could do

ABOVE *Soul Train* simultaneously encompassed days gone by, with appearances by Redd, and contemporary phenomena, like break dancing. **LEFT** Herbie Hancock creates a whole new sound in Episode 431.

during an instrumental piece when you're not playing for real. The addition of Grandmaster DST to his performance gave credibility to hip-hop as an art form. Suddenly "turntablism" equated to "the needle on the record." Seeing a DJ using cutting as an instrument really changed the lives for those watching and made the turntable a bona fide instrument. It was damn near revolutionary.

Herbie hailed from a vast history of jazz musicianship, most famously with his band the Headhunters, which is when he began to feed his fusion of funk and jazz music to voracious audiences. Fishing in deeper waters, he left the band behind and infused his ready-made fun into hip-hop waters, the result of which is the *Future Shock* album, which spawned "Rockit," the most important musical development of the hip-hop era. The single immediately turned Herbie into a b-boy hero and an MTV staple, pulling a David and Goliath on *Thriller* as it took home the award for best concept video at the first MTV awards.

Of course, Herbie didn't appear in the video; that was not advised back then. There was concern that having a black man in the video would impede it from getting airtime, so the directors of the video, Kevin Godley and Lol Creme (former members of the pop outfit 10cc), used futuristic-looking mannequins instead.

THE BIG MOMENTS

192 | SOUL TRAIN

OPPOSITE TOP Gregory Hines lends his class, charisma, and multitudes of talent to the show in Episode 586 on December 10, 1988. **OPPOSITE BOTTOM LEFT** Mr. T never addressed Don as "fool." **OPPOSITE BOTTOM RIGHT** Grace Jones in Episode 528. **ABOVE** They're baaack . . . Kool & the Gang.

Kool & the Gang

Sometimes a victory can be bittersweet, and Kool & the Gang's performance in Episode 432 on December 17, 1983, was just that. This urban group had aspirations of pop superstardom, and ultimately no group from the '70s better represented the evolution of the dream than them. Even Don pulled no punches during the interview by saying, "You've come a long way from 'Jungle Boogie.'" The blatant callout of the loss of their funkiness was the bitter part of this victory lap. Most loyal fans frowned on the crossover dreams of the '80s. But Kool & the Gang miraculously managed to land with both feet on solid ground unscathed, performing "Joanna" and "Tonight" from the *In the Heart* album. This made many from *Soul Train*'s "older" generation (that would include my Aunt Sharon) give the show a second look.

THE BIG MOMENTS | 193

A Salute to Diana Ross

Diana Ross left Motown in '81, but her celebrity status stayed just as magnatic in the 1980s as it was in the '60s. Although her first RCA Records album *Why Do Fools Fall in Love*, which she promoted on *Soul Train*, didn't sell as well as the self-titled album before, it featured the incomparable ballad of the century, "Endless Love," and a few other hits, written by *Soul Train* blue-eyed soul vets, Michael Sembello ("Mirror Mirror") and Dan Hartman ("It's Never Too Late"). In Episode 382 on January 30, 1982, Don rolled out the red carpet for Diana, and didn't bother to introduce her before she opened the show with "It's Never Too Late." Some people need no introductions.

A Note about New Jack— and Don Dancing

Between 1984 and 1986, the floodgates opened for fusion music styles. Blended soul and hip-hop emerged after Chaka Khan became the first R&B artist to collaborate with a guest rapper, which she did on her hit "I Feel for You," a hip-hop-friendly song with harder dance beats.

Lisa Lisa and Cult Jam's Episode 500 on April 12, 1986, and Full Force's appearance a week later in Episode 501 further dem-

TOP Diana Ross in Episode 382. **ABOVE** Lisa Lisa is "All Cried Out" in 1986.

ABOVE Full Force performed "Love Is for Suckers." **RIGHT** Chaka takes hold of new jack swing.

onstrated yet another stage of the evolution of black music. Before music mogul Teddy Riley was officially credited with the creation of new jack swing, it was Brooklyn's Full Force that planted the seeds. The quick beats of their percussion were ones that could easily be rhymed over and sung to. And while new jack swing was defined by its use of drums, it did not pick up on the trend of using sampled beats, and instead created beats using the then new SP-1200 and Roland TR-808 drum machines. These also created the sound that would come from the hip-hop "swing" beats.

When they appeared on *Soul Train* on April 19, 1986, the production team made a major faux pas: Sid McCoy failed to announce Full Force as a guest on the show. (Watching the telecast, this made me think they were added at the last minute.) Despite being left out of the show's legendary introduction, they went on to present one of the most notable a cappella moments of any interview. You could tell by Don's reaction that he was instantly elated with the group as they sang thirty seconds of their hit "Alice, I Want You Just for Me!" The energy of this spontaneous jam completely fed the crowd and compelled Don to do something he never did in an interview—dance. You could tell the singers knew they had a limited time to make a good impression and they made the most of it. What started off as a mundane interview ended with an ambush that told Don, "We dance, we sing, we produce." From that moment on, Don and Full Force were like family.

The Cult of Personality

While the late '80s still had much to offer to the music world, considering hip-hop's momentum as well as the rise of new jack swing and Janet Jackson utilizing the new jack swing sound to prepare to take over the title of pop goddess, the advent of video added a second dimension to one's music experience. Musicianship and singing weren't the only basic requirements. Because of the high standard set by Michael Jackson, a performer's visual presentation had to match or, in some cases, surpass sound presentation (and for most artists who ruled the tops of the charts in the late '80s, that certainly rang true). Nuance, tone, and delivery were no longer lauded, but a display of agility, a physical aesthetic, and an all-encompassing magnetism could get an artist everywhere. It was all about presentation as opposed to three minutes and thirty seconds on a turntable. Welcome to the dawn of the cult of personality, where persona was the selling tool.

Soul Train managed to weather the storm of many phases of music using its blueprint. The closest that any one television program got to capturing *Soul Train*'s lightning in a bottle was *Yo! MTV Raps,* which paralleled *Soul Train*'s formula for presenting music and culture. First aired in 1988, the show, much like the first three years of *Soul Train*, was able to one-up its predecessor by presenting an obscure lifestyle to black children *and* white children and all stops in between.

THE BIG MOMENTS

ABOVE Paula Abdul comes out from behind the scenes in Episode 578 on October 15, 1988. **OPPOSITE TOP** Even in 1989, for Don the show was still about dancing. **OPPOSITE BOTTOM LEFT** When Kim Fields—known for her role of Tootie Ramsey on *The Facts of Life*—sang her 1984 ode to Michael Jackson, "Dear Michael," in Episode 450 on June 23, 1984, it was a "Did I just see that?" moment for me. **OPPOSITE BOTTOM RIGHT** Don and Keenan Ivory Wayans admiring the iconic *Soul Train* sign in Episode 589 on January 28, 1989.

Similar to the effect that the Johnson commercials had on the '70s youth, hip-hop videos and interview segments with Fab 5 Freddy affected style, lingo, dances, and swagger. An entirely new Afrocentric culture for a widespread audience was born from it. In the late '80s *Soul Train* had to fully embrace hip-hop culture as if it were an old comfortable shoe. It was no longer a novelty or a treat that would appear once every nine episodes when Don had a hip-hop booking. The exception had become the rule.

The End of the Decade

By the end of the 1980s, *Soul Train* was no longer the word-of-mouth, fringe secret of all tastemakers and hit makers. The underground subculture had fully blossomed into the gold standard of performance and culture, holding its own next to its competition of the day—*Yo! MTV Raps*, the *Arsenio Hall Show*, and *American Bandstand*—and then quietly outlasting them all.

On the cusp of the 1990s, the show's legacy and history was still held holy by fans who grew up with the show and were now a part of it. More of a household name than ever, *Soul Train* was accessed by millions of homes. Beginning in 1985, Don enjoyed his highest ratings, with Nielsen ratings showing that 6.1 percent of American homes watched it, which is unheard of for a variety show. (Typically a late-night talk show gets more like 2.8/2.9, indicating that 2.8 or 2.9 percent of the population tunes in.)

Despite the show's plethora of changes in music, video, cable, technology, and demographics, Don still had a grip on the jugular vein of pop culture and entertainment. *Soul Train* hadn't run out of steam. In its dust it left behind the era of "I think I can" and motored confidently into the "I-*know*-I-can" decade of the '90s.

THE IDEA

The up-and-coming bands of the 1980s, the ones who had become like nieces and nephews to Don Cornelius, took a cue from his entrepreneurial spirit and worked their way to the summit of the music industry of the nineties. Janet Jackson got a star on the Hollywood Walk of Fame and was crowned pop princess, leading her rhythm nation into the era of new jack swing. Michael Bivins provided management and guidance to future *Soul Train* performers Boyz II Men and Another Bad Creation. Albert Brown, better known as Al B. Sure!, mentored future Jodeci member DeVante Swing, who, in turn, mentored future *Soul Train* performers Missy Elliott and Timbaland. Songwriters like Babyface and Teddy Riley and managers like Russell Simmons became leading producers and label execs. And Quincy Jones was a god.

202 SOUL TRAIN

The Soul Train *legacy and brand are of utmost importance to me and to* Soul Train's *millions of fans. After years of offers, I feel the time is now finally right to pass the torch.*

—Don Cornelius

Even twenty years after its inception, *Soul Train* hadn't lost its original vision of bringing quality black entertainment, style, fashion, music, and dance into the living rooms of millions of viewers. Its initial basement-party feel had blossomed into a plush nightclub atmosphere. Integration was at an all-time high, which made *Soul Train* not just a showcase of Afrocentricity, but a utopian clubhouse for every ethnic group with a common love of rhythmic expression and style that now tuned in to watch the show.

For me, the stars of *Soul Train* in the 1990s were the scantily clad dancers—the sexiest women of the show's history. The focus was less on new dances—even though there were still plenty for me to learn now that I was about to turn club age—and more on the conveyor belt of eye candy.

As a production fanatic, though, I also took notice of the new opening animation. To me, it felt as if the show became overwhelming—lots of digital camera effects, too many lights, diminished power of the iconic logo in the center of the room, and other nitpicky unmentionables. What it lacked in its long-running tradition, however, *Soul Train* gained in other areas—or did it? Without question, this decade was a major turning point in the show. But were women now being objectified? Did *Soul Train* suddenly become the establishment that it was once against? The answer is quite possibly. But to paraphrase D'Angelo's "Devil's Pie," *Who am I to judge the evil that I religiously supported every Saturday?*

Soul Train's third decade never experienced a talent drought, though, and the flow of talent helped balance out the more liberal changes. Established names Kool & the Gang, Stevie Wonder, the O'Jays, and Quincy Jones held court with even harder-to-obtain A-list talent who finally made their debut appearances on

PAGE 200 Quincy Jones worked his way to the top, performing in the third spot in Episode 160 on November 29, 1975. **OPPOSITE TOP** Boyz II Men with Don in Episode 667 on June 1, 1991. **OPPOSITE BOTTOM** No matter how far we'd come from the first decade of *Soul Train*, the Line was still the dancers' time to shine.

TEEMING THEMES

Soul Train used various theme songs during its run.

- 1971–1973: "*Soul Train* (Hot Potato)" by King Curtis (Curtis Ousley), later redone by the Rimshots as "*Soul Train*, Parts 1 & 2."
- 1973–1975: "TSOP (The Sound of Philadelphia)," composed by Gamble & Huff and performed by Philadelphia soul studio group MFSB with vocals by the Three Degrees. The song became a radio hit in 1974 and is the show's best-known theme.
- 1975–1976: "*Soul Train* '75" by the Soul Train Gang.
- 1976–1978: "*Soul Train* '76 (Get on Board)," also by the Soul Train Gang.
- 1978–1980: "*Soul Train* Theme '79" by the Hollywood Disco Jazz Band with vocals by the Waters.
- 1980–1983: "Up on *Soul Train*," first by the Waters and later by the Whispers, whose version is on their 1980 album *Imagination*.
- 1983–1987: "*Soul Train*'s a Comin'" by O'Bryan.
- 1987–1989: "TSOP '87," a remake of the original "TSOP," composed and produced by George Duke.
- 1989–1993: "TSOP '89," a remixed version, also by Duke.
- 1993–1999: "*Soul Train* '93" (Know You Like to Dance) by Naughty by Nature.
- 2000–2006: "TSOP 200," by Dr. Freeze with rap vocals by hip-hop artist Samson.

the show, including Prince, Lenny Kravitz, and Mariah Carey, not to mention the record breakers and the future establishment that came to rule this decade: Boyz II Men, TLC, Snoop Dogg, Mary J. Blige, and Destiny's Child.

Meditations on the Theme

In 1991, I was still recording *Soul Train* every week on my VCR, even though I was personally dismayed that Don dropped the O'Bryan theme and went back to the TSOP theme—the iconic 1974 song—redone with George Duke. It may have seemed clever at the time, but I say never touch a classic, because the new version only pales in comparison. In celebration of its twentieth anniversary, *Soul Train* was entering self-congratulation mode. Sid McCoy changed the script of his iconic intro, no longer letting us know that *Soul Train* was the "hippest trip in America." Instead, Sid gave us the historical facts: "the longest-running first-run

THE IDEA   203

syndicated show in television history." But coming from Sid's mouth, the superfluous factoid still sounded cool. For the first couple '90s seasons, he opted to boast only of the show's record-setting significance, but soon added "and the hippest trip in America."

This also marked the first time in the show's twenty years that the tag animation didn't scare me. Or maybe I had finally grown up.

The Decade-Defining Sound

Hip-hop acts had the chance to add their shine to *Soul Train* in the '90s, but new jack was the type of music that *Soul Train* could wholeheartedly embrace because there were enough soul elements fused in the music to justify its utilization on the show. Two performers-turned-pacesetters would use the *Soul Train* platform to expand new jack swing into the decade's defining sound—Babyface and Teddy Riley.

BABYFACE

Babyface was first a guest on *Soul Train* on Episode 450 in 1984 as the keyboard player for the Solar Records band the Deele (a funk band out of Cincinnati), and then in 1986 broke out as a solo performer with his debut album, *Lovers*. But it wasn't until the ushering in of new jack swing in the late '80s that he ruled with an iron fist.

Using highly adult-themed lyrics, Babyface's brand of new jack swing had the feel of adult contemporary. It had the bounce of new jack swing without the additives and preservatives. Babyface slowly morphed from sideman to songwriter for fellow Solar acts, most notably the Whispers, to give them the ticket to their last trip to the top ten pop charts with "Rock Steady" in 1987. After that, the doors flung wide open for Babyface, and he began writing, producing, and cultivating the new jack swing culture for the likes of Karyn White, Paula Abdul, Pebbles, and Whitney Houston. His little ditty for Boyz II Men, "End of the Road," was the tipping point to him partnering with L.A. Reid, the former Deele drummer, to form their own label, LaFace. They forged acts TLC, Toni Braxton, P!nk, and Usher, giving Babyface access to every artist in the stratosphere from Michael Jackson to Madonna and Eric Clapton to Phil Collins. Babyface holds the distinct honor of winning the most consecutive Producer of the Year Grammys (three) for his work between 1995 and 1997. Boyz II Men, Brandy, Bobby Brown, Tevin Campbell, Michael Bolton, Patti LaBelle, Faith Evans, and Sheena Easton were a few of his 1990s conquests.

Babyface was a quadruple threat—songwriter, producer, manager, and CEO of LaFace, which gave him the ability to cast such a wide net in the sea of entertainment. Many of his artists and song creations ruled the '90s performances of *Soul Train*. He provided the show with half its output and soundtracks for a good part of the decade. The other half came from Teddy Riley.

OPPOSITE TOP As a performer, Babyface met Don in 1987 in Episode 545. **OPPOSITE BOTTOM** In 1987, before he began his own label, Babyface sang "I Love You Baby" and "Chivalry." **TOP** LaFace Records launched TLC. **BOTTOM LEFT** Usher in 1997 performing "You Make Me Wanna." **BOTTOM RIGHT** Hey, Usher! They told you to "be a showman," not, "show, man."

THE IDEA

TEDDY RILEY

Teddy Riley had as equal a footing in '90s culture as Babyface, and possibly even booked more acts on *Soul Train*. Babyface was the clean-cut Beatles to Riley's dirty Stones. As one-third of the band Guy, Teddy was the keyboardist and mastermind as the primary producer and songwriter. He took his drum machine production experience and filtered it through hip-hop, providing the music with its most defining element—louder drums than traditional melodic music. His traditional musicianship training gave him an advantage over other producers because he could play keyboards *and* the drum programs. Think about it this way. Hip-hop is 90 percent drum programming, 5 percent sampled sound sources, and 5 percent musicianship. Teddy evened out the playing field by giving 33.3 percent to drum, 33.3 percent to sampling, and 33.3 percent to musicianship. This made fans of more traditional music (and hip-hop naysayers) enraptured by Teddy's brand, and were highly important to the sound and development of Guy. Lead singer Aaron Hall was not nondescript, but Teddy's musical concoction was so potent that it didn't need a costar.

Teddy began as an unknown producer for acts like Kool Moe Dee and Doug E. Fresh & the Get Fresh Crew. Later, because of his connection to the famous Harlem club, the Rooftop, owned by his uncle, almost all of his clientele came through there—Heavy D & the Boyz, Keith Sweat, and, most important, Bobby Brown. Bobby was Teddy's first act to match LaFace's adult contemporary brand of new jack swing with the bull's-eye album, *Don't Be Cruel* (seven million records sold). That opened the door for Teddy's biggest project, producing Michael Jackson's *Dangerous* album. He then mentored two young apprentices in 1990, Pharrell Williams and Chad Hugo. By the time they were ready to leave Teddy's nest, they were established stars in their own right as members of the Neptunes. Teddy moved on to form BLACKstreet. Coincidentally, BLACKstreet performed on *Soul Train* in Episode 733 on June 19, 1993, the episode before Don's last show as host.

OPPOSITE TOP LEFT The Deele in Episode 558, whose drummer, L.A. Reid, would become the other half of LaFace Records. **OPPOSITE TOP RIGHT** Doug E. Fresh in Episode 599 on May 6, 1989. **OPPOSITE BOTTOM** Guy was the third act in Episode 571 on May 28, 1988. **TOP** Slated in second position out of three acts, Guy returns in Episode 589 on January 28, 1989. **LEFT** Bobby Brown.

THE IDEA

THE ACTS

Okay, smarty, when *Soul Train* kicked off the nineties, it was technically still 1989. But when Young MC performed his explosive hit "Bust a Move" in Episode 611 on October 21, 1989, Don could hear the future. Fortune was smiling on *Soul Train*; hip-hop acts were showing up onscreen at the same time they were selling albums like crazy. The decade would turn into a showdown between new jack and hip-hop, and Young MC appealed to both camps. The feel-good hit-maker of the year, he stood in third place in the show's performance lineup, following the R&B singer and former Atlantic Starr frontwoman Sharon Bryant and the wistful blue-eyed soul singer Michael Bolton.

PAGE 208 Big Daddy Kane in Episode 681 on November 30, 1991. **TOP LEFT** Young MC in Episode 611 on October 21, 1989. **ABOVE LEFT** Michael Bolton, also in Episode 611, is a "Soul Provider" in Season 19. **TOP RIGHT** Color Me Badd in Episode 674. **ABOVE RIGHT** Peabo Bryson. **OPPOSITE TOP** DJ Jazzy Jeff & the Fresh Prince. **OPPOSITE BOTTOM** Public Enemy becomes a household name in Episode 682 on December 7, 1991.

> Soul Train *was developed as a radio show on television. It was the radio show that I always wanted and never had.*
>
> —Don Cornelius

OPPOSITE TOP Kid 'n Play in Episode 635 on June 2, 1990. **OPPOSITE BOTTOM** Run-D.M.C. in Episode 660 on March 16, 1991. **ABOVE** Underage hip-hoppers Kris Kross in Episode 696 on May 9, 1992. **LEFT** Ice-T pays tribute to Quincy Jones in Episode 643 on October 20, 1990.

THE ACTS | 213

ABOVE The Beastie Boys.

Back to Beastie

Episode 621 on January 27, 1990, marked a notable appearance by the Beastie Boys. Though they were written off as a one-time novelty act, the album they promoted on this episode, *Paul's Boutique,* turned out to be one of the greatest critically lauded recordings in pop music history. I count this appearance as a victory lap for the Beastie Boys, for they actually crafted an exclusive *Soul Train* version of their song "Shadrach." It's a personal favorite episode of mine because when the Roots made an appearance in Episode 946 on March 4, 2000, we too crafted an exclusive *Soul Train* version of our performances to make them appear as if we were doing them live. Just as the Beastie Boys did before us, we went into the studio the night before our *Soul Train* performance. We redid "You Got Me" with Jill Scott and "What You Want" with Jaguar Wright.

The Beastie Boys remixed "Shadrach" and used *Soul Train*–specific lyrics about Don. When I asked them about his episode, they explained that they didn't want to go down in lip-sync history, since they were embarrassed by their debut appearance in Episode 527 in 1987. So to right a wrong, they went into the studio and cut an original for the show. The audience was very into it, but Don seemed rather unmoved by their "Ode to Don," even during the interview section when they were talking about their admiration for the show, having grown up with it. This was when I first started to think this might be Don's last stop on the train. When an effort like "Shadrach" could be so well put together yet lost on him, I couldn't help but wonder if it might be downhill from there.

Bell Biv DeVoe

It's a good thing Bell Biv DeVoe could swoop in and offer Don the light of paternal pride, as they did in Episode 628 on April 14, 1990. The biggest question of the summer of 1990 was, "How did the three lesser members of New Edition wind up becoming the anchor of an institution?" "Poison" was *the* dance jam of the summer, and much like during Jody Watley's first solo performance in Episode 525 in 1986, I actually felt Don's enthusiasm sing through. He was like an uncle watching his rambunctious nephews turn into men. This is really where BBD's seasoning and experience shined through. Because no unit could ever dance as well as New Edition could in R&B music, Bell Biv DeVoe set the standard in upholding the Motown torch while adding personality to it.

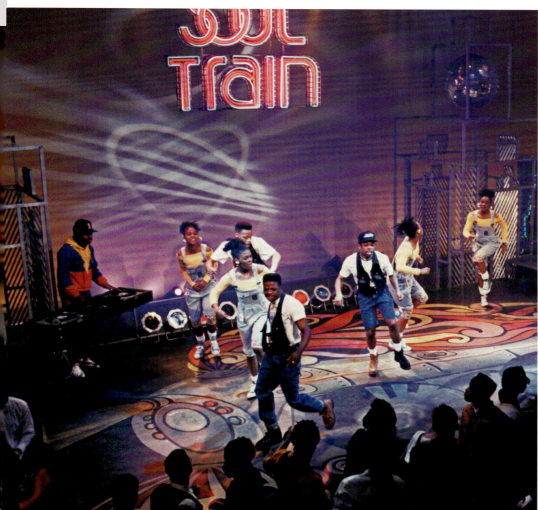

ABOVE LEFT Bell Biv DeVoe. **ABOVE RIGHT** Lenny Kravitz.

It was also in this episode that I received a clue of what an average *Soul Train* taping was like. I liked the behind-the-music feel that I hadn't gotten before from the show, at least since the Cholly Atkins/O'Jays Episode 153 back in 1975. During the interview, Ronnie DeVoe admitted to the home audience, "Y'all don't know how hard this is. This is like our third time doing this song." This was a rare break of the wall in explaining how the show runs: in order to get the taping just right, the performers might have to go through the song multiple times, without looking tired. Don gave praise to the out-of-breath trio, saying, "You work hard up there."

Lenny Kravitz

When I turned on *Soul Train* on November 2, 1991, to watch Episode 677, it was my intent to "see it to believe it." Was Don really going to embrace an alternative black act? By this point in his career, Lenny Kravitz was more than just a household name in my home—he was a certified international sensation. Through the press, Lenny had voiced his frustration with being rejected by black radio, so his *Soul Train* booking was a small but sweet victory.

Lenny performed from "Mama Said," his Curtis Mayfield–flavored single, and his Earth, Wind & Fire derivative, "What Goes Around Comes Around." This was actually Lenny's second appearance on *Soul Train*. At twenty years old, he was a keytar player in Herb Alpert's 1984 appearance on Episode 462.

Lenny humorously fumed at this factoid when I happily exposed it on Twitter on my birthday in 2013.

Back in 1984, Lenny looked like a male model, nothing close to the hippie love child he had come to be. He wasn't even Lenny Kravitz then—he went by "Romeo Blue" before he realized his given name was actually a better stage name.

It wouldn't be until 1989 that Lenny would come forward looking and sounding very different, pioneering a left-of-center alternative sound. This was a coup for Don because by 1991 Lenny was a platinum act. In Don's eyes, booking Lenny made sense from a business standpoint. In 1993, Lenny unleashed *Are You Gonna Go My Way*, and there was no need to return to *Soul Train* to promote that album, or any other for that matter.

THE ACTS

SOUL SURVIVORS

Many of the marquee *Soul Train* acts reestablished their positions in the second-tier spot, including Ready for the World (Episode 674), S.O.S. Band (Episode 680), and Atlantic Starr (Episode 681). Although Don didn't close the door to his established acts that had enjoyed headlining *Soul Train* for decades, the trend for these acts, who were struggling to find their voice in the '90s, was to take a backseat to a bigger headlining act. Others included the Main Ingredient (Episode 619), Lakeside (Episode 641), Brenda Russell (Episode 646), LeVert (Episode 649), Jeffrey Osborne (Episode 653), Gerald Alston (Episode 659), and 5 Star (Episode 665).

ABOVE Isaac Hayes and Barry White. **LEFT** The S.O.S. Band in Episode 680 on November 23, 1991. **BELOW** Ziggy Marley & the Melody Makers in Episode 682 on December 7, 1991. **OPPOSITE** Barry White in Episode 687 on February 8, 1992.

Alternative Black Music

Episodes 675 and 682 were notable for performances by the Brand New Heavies and Ziggy Marley and the Melody Makers, respectively. Both acts formed different branches of the soul tree, with Ziggy being part of the lineage of the great Bob Marley, and the Brand New Heavies being the pioneers of the acid jazz movement in London. Once acid jazz made its way to America, it was rechristened as neo soul, the branch that the Roots would expand upon.

Classic Collaboration

Barry White and Isaac Hayes made a historic appearance on *Soul Train* in Episode 687 on February 8, 1992. It was amazing to see the two pioneers of '70s disco finally sharing a billing as "Barry White with Isaac Hayes." These two were often categorized together because they were the first to utilize lush orchestral stings, and were known for "baby-making" music. This episode marked the official iconic gathering of two institutions, without whom the progression of soul would have had a hard time finding its own path.

THE MOVES

I used the first decade of *Soul Train* for education and the second decade for entertainment. In the '90s, I was getting ready to hit the clubs, and that meant paying special attention to the one aspect of the show that had stayed constant all those years: the *Soul Train* Line and its dancers. The fellas were cool, the women were sexy, and the Line was unconditionally engaging. I studied the dancers with a new eye, aware that I was about to take my dance party on the road.

There was something vulnerable about the Line, and it had everything to do with the fact that it's extremely difficult to do a dance routine while walking forward. Most dancing is done in one spot, so to walk and dance while still holding the attention of your audience is no easy feat. The *Soul Train* Line was where you'd find the dancers at their most daring. And even when an idea wasn't executed well, points were still given for effort.

The Backup Moves Up Front

In the '90s, all the R&B artists on the show seemed to emerge from the new jack swing branch or had changed their approach to fit the new format. Part of that approach was seen in the dance and presentation of the acts, as displayed through the sudden influx of backup dancers accompanying artists when they performed on the show. In the '70s and '80s, dancers were a treat because they were rarely utilized for song performances, but in the '90s, it was standard to have them. This is precisely why new jack swing provided much-needed energy and enthusiasm for the show's dancers. MC Hammer, Boyz II Men, Jodeci, and even long-standing hip-hop vets like Big Daddy Kane, Chubb Rock, Bobby Brown, and LL Cool J stepped up their dancing games and led the audience into near moshing mode. As far as crowd enthusiasm was concerned, the display of excitement took on a new shape, often molded by Louie Carr.

What was also quite exciting for the dancers coming on the show to be "discovered" was the return of former *Soul Train* dancer Jeffrey Daniel to tout his solo career. In Episode 632 on May 12, 1990, Jeffrey offered another round of hope to a slew of pupils.

Meet the Cast

SALLY ACHENBACH

With a foot planted in each decade, Sally came into her own in the '90s. As she grew up, she earned more camera time, and it wasn't only because she was a terrific dancer. It was also because she was one of the most enthusiastic of the group. She didn't work the camera like some other dancers did, or at least it seemed that way because she was so natural. During an interview I once heard her give, she said that she was there purely for the fun of it. And you could tell that was the truth. The girl next door mixed with the perfect dose of confidence, Sally was serious about having fun. When she danced, you felt like she was in the room with you, totally accessible. You know when you just know a person is cool? To me, that's Sally.

PAGE 218 A homage to biker shorts. PAGES 220–221 *Soul Train* still featured its famed dance segments; however, in my opinion, spontaneity and novelty were things of the past. OPPOSITE BOTTOM RIGHT Dancer Jeffrey Daniel. OPPOSITE TOP Sally Achenbach. OPPOSITE BOTTOM LEFT Even George Jefferson brought backup dancers with him. ABOVE Debbie Allen stunned us all when she stunned Don. TOP I love this shot because it encapsulates the feeling of *Soul Train*—a lot of love, camaraderie, and fun, as Debbie Allen plants one on Heavy D with stage manager Reggie Rutherford sharing the moment.

CARMEN ELECTRA

On the other hand, the Prince-discovered Carmen Electra was a shock to the system. It is said that Prince took notice and interest in small-town Tara Leigh Patrick from Sharonville, Ohio, on a *Soul Train* episode and renamed her. The rest, as they say, is history.

BARBARA SCOTT

If you were to look up "sexy sophisticate" in the dictionary, you'd find Barbara in a variety of skirt-and-jacket combinations buttoned up with a little bit of nasty. She could also rock a catsuit like nobody's business and do her thing. Watching her dance, I was reminded of what Don wanted his dancers to represent: self-respect, rhythm, and eternal youth.

DEBBIE ALLEN*

(Although not a regular, I'll give her honorary status.) When it came to showing dancers the potential they had to make waves in all forms of entertainment and pop culture, the illustrious Debbie Allen raised the bar and then some. Debbie visited the show on September 23, 1989, and gave a performance to which Don conceded: "This being the 607th episode of this show, in its twentieth year, I have to acknowledge that that was one of the best performances I have ever seen." At this point Debbie was in her forties and directing *A Different World*, but she could still sweep across a dance floor to stun a man who had literally seen it all.

THE MOVES

THE BIG MOMENTS

As I pored over the episode lists of the 1990s, I was struck by how many of the big moments were throwbacks to the early days of the show, and by extension to the good old days of soul music. Many of the most compelling shows were tributes to icons who had started out as working musicians, and whose appearances on the show had helped them grow into icons. I also noticed how balanced the show had become, gender-wise: by the nineties, *Soul Train* was a consistent and reliable showcase for the rising female forces of hip-hop and soul. But perhaps the biggest moment of them all came without warning.

PAGE 224 After a hiatus from the show, Stevie Wonder rings in Season 21 in 1991. **TOP** Both heroes to their public, Quincy Jones and Don talk shop. **BOTTOM** All the top hip-hop stars came to pay tribute to Quincy Jones, including Kool Moe Dee and Ice-T.

Tribute to Quincy Jones

Episode 643 was definitely a nice surprise for me and one of the better shows of the 1990s. On October 20, 1990, *Soul Train* celebrated Quincy Jones's thirty-five years in music with an all-star tribute. It was probably the most star-studded show ever, with Kool Moe Dee, Melly Mel, Ice-T, and Big Daddy Kane (they were all there to celebrate the *Back on the Block* album), along with El DeBarge, the Winans, Al B. Sure!, Siedah Garrett, and Tevin Campbell. The show also featured clips of Quincy's documentary *Listen Up*. In this one episode, Don managed to cram in dancing to Quincy's hit songs; airing the Chaka Khan and Ray Charles video of their 1990 remake of Quincy's 1976 "I'll be Good to You," originally performed by the Brothers Johnson; having serious one-on-one time in two very long interview segments with Don; and celebrities singing in Quincy's honor. I call this episode "a great day on *Soul Train*."

ABOVE It's déjà vu all over again, as the audience sings a new *Soul Train* theme song with Stevie Wonder. **RIGHT** Don was really relishing this moment with Stevie.

Tribute to Stevie Wonder

The debut episode of Season 21 on September 21, 1991, is my other top pick from the '90s. Episode 671 was a tribute to Stevie Wonder. First coming aboard in *Soul Train*'s second year to help out the show in its fledgling stage, Stevie returned eighteen years later for a reunion of iconic artists. It was nice to see Stevie and Don together again; it felt like Stevie had returned home. This episode marked a unique time when an artist who had become bigger than the show decided to visit again. As Don displayed what had become rare signs of brotherly affection and happiness, it seemed like he couldn't contain his enthusiasm. He was almost in tears and even kissed Stevie on the top of his head.

Stevie performed tracks off his *Jungle Fever* soundtrack and conducted three long interview segments with a live piano. As Wonder-esque as ever, he sang an impromptu live medley of his hits, similar to the first two times he was on the show. As a gift to the generation who had witnessed Stevie's previous *Soul Train* appearances—as well as to the generation who hadn't yet experienced them—Don aired the clip from Episode 46 in 1973 of Stevie singing his version of the *Soul Train* theme song. When they cut back to the present, Stevie was surrounded by the dancers, a re-creation of the iconic moment. The younger kids were singing the songs as loud, or louder, than Stevie, which brought the show full circle. And then he outdid himself. Stevie turned "Superstition" into another *Soul Train* theme song and closed the show while singing to the credits, "Time to get on Soul Train, time to get on board."

 A guy like me can't be doing the 'love, peace, and soul!' shtick for the rest of his life until people start to say, 'What's he doing that for?' You gotta know when to get out.

—Don Cornelius

THE BIG MOMENTS

Tribute to Gladys Knight

It was sentimental when Gladys Knight came back for her tribute show on October 5, 1991. Don was sure to pass on to each generation of his viewers the fact that she was the very first performer on the show. For Episode 673, Gladys returned almost twenty years to the day from the inaugural episode on October 2, 1971. I'm sure the apropos timing was planned. Don always let it be known on all her shows that he hosted (she made seven appearances from 1971 to 1993) that "if it weren't for Gladys Knight, none of this would be here." What is probably most notable about this appearance is that Gladys had a hit with the Calloway brothers at the time called "Love Overboard," so she wasn't riding off the fumes of her past. She and the Pips had a top five R&B hit on their hands and were still showing the way.

OPPOSITE LEFT On May 4, 1974, Gladys Knight & the Pips performed five of their hits: "Neither One of Us," "Midnight Train to Georgia," "You're the Best Thing That Ever Happened to Me," "I Got to Use My Imagination," and "On and On." **LEFT** Gladys Knight, in Episode 33 on September 23, 1972, had reached icon status at the astonishingly young age of twenty-seven. **BELOW** They started it all in Episode 1: Gladys Knight & the Pips return in Episode 33. **BOTTOM** Coming full circle, Gladys Knight & the Pips are given a tribute show in Episode 564 on April 9, 1988.

THE BIG MOMENTS

Gerald and Eddie Levert

Episode 690 could've been called 360, since it was literally full circle, as two of my favorite Leverts—father Eddie and son Gerald—had a go-round with Don. The history here was thick, not only between Don and Eddie, but between Eddie and his son, whom Eddie helped to become a star. Eddie called in every favor and leveraged every resource in order to see his son's ambitions reached. And by February 29, 1992, Gerald's success had eclipsed his father's. By that time, Gerald's celebrity was due to a wave of top five hits: "Casanova," "Pop, Goes My Mind," "My Forever Love," "Sweet Sensation," "Addicted to You," "Just Coolin'," and "Baby I'm Ready." Now father needed son, and where better to show off as a collaborative team, performing together, than on *Soul Train*.

Move to Movies

Episode 679 on November 16, 1991, was different beyond compare because the show was dedicated to the successful movie brought to us by Doug McHenry and George Jackson, *House Party 2*. Don introduced the show as a "tribute to the *House Party* soundtrack." This episode is the actual manifestation of the *Soul Train* domino effect. In paying tribute to *House Party 2*, Don was giving a homecoming to his offspring—the new onslaught of black executive producers, directors, and writers who were making an above-the-radar impact in the mainstream. With *Soul Train* being the original medium credited with opening doors for such behind-the-scenes African American talent, this was a kiss-the-ring-worthy moment. The show was in line with Quincy Jones's episode of the prior season, with artists Kid 'n Play, Tony! Toni! Toné!, and Ralph Tresvant performing tracks off the soundtrack, except now Don was saluting a product instead of a person.

Introducing Girl Power

Soul Train gave women a platform that enabled them to be taken more seriously than ever as forces in music and performance, particularly as soul music rediscovered its identity in the early '90s. After the way was paved by the fearless Salt-N-Pepa, women planted a flag on the planet of hip-hop. TLC, Queen Latifah, and Mary J. Blige debuted in all their edgy glory and became the eminent women of the '90s. Soul music found its footing again through the blending of hip-hop aesthetics with traditional soul singing and presentation. As a result, the golden pipes of Mariah Carey, CeCe Peniston, Toni Braxton, Vanessa Williams, and En Vogue swept through the *Soul Train* set like an effervescent breeze blowing crisp life into an industry that traditionalists tsk-tsked and swore off as artistically dead.

REGINA BELLE

Regina Belle even set new standards for Disney's animated movie soundtracks on *Soul Train*. She performed *Aladdin*'s "A Whole New World" with Peabo Bryson in Episode 725 on March 27, 1993.

JODY RETURNS

Episode 627 on April 7, 1990, marked the return of Jody Watley for her third appearance as a solo artist. By this point, she had won her Grammy for "Best New Artist," spreading more hope among the female members of the audience.

EN VOGUE

On May 19, 1990, En Vogue, the *it* girl group of the '90s, second to TLC, graced *Soul Train* with their presence. R&B had a severe identity problem in the '80s, and it wasn't until new jack swing, when the union of gospel singing and hip-hop beats solidified, that R&B started to find its footing again. As a result, a slew of groups that looked hip-hop while sounding R&B were born. When En Vogue performed "Hold On" in Episode 633, the first forty-five seconds of Smokey Robinson's "Who's Loving You" in a cappella served as a reminder that, *yes, we're using hip-hop aesthetics to get our point across, but we are first and foremost singers.*

SALT-N-PEPA

Salt-N-Pepa maintained their status as the most iconic female act in hip-hop when they appeared on *Soul Train* in Episode 646 on November 10, 1990. With their platinum hit "Push It," they were already megastars by this time.

ABOVE "A Whole New World," performed by Regina Bell and Peabo Bryson. **OPPOSITE TOP LEFT** Another full-circle moment is created when savvy sophisticate Jody Watley returns to the show; she continued to inspire hopeful viewers with dreams. **OPPOSITE BOTTOM LEFT** En Vogue. **OPPOSITE TOP RIGHT** Salt-N-Pepa. **OPPOSITE BOTTOM RIGHT** Vanessa Williams.

VANESSA WILLIAMS

You couldn't help but marvel at Vanessa Williams in Episode 684 on January 18, 1992. She was brains and beauty, but most importantly, her talent was an example for anyone who has ever been the underdog. As she performed her hard-earned hits, including "Save the Best for Last," Vanessa proved that pure solid-gold talent could withstand any tabloid scandal.

THE BIG MOMENTS

Vision of Mariah

Artists didn't usually come to the show when they were on the rise or already megastars, unless the megastars were on the brink of slipping. But in the case of Mariah Carey, her then husband and Svengali manager, Tommy Mottola, wisely booked her a stop on *Soul Train*. I say wisely because it was a way for Mariah to show gratitude and respect to the audience that had supported her. With five number one hits behind her, she was already established well beyond the typical reach of *Soul Train* by Episode 688 on February 15, 1992, but arrived anyway to sing "Emotions."

ABOVE Just shy of her twenty-second birthday, Mariah Carey already had the goods and then some. **OPPOSITE TOP** Lisa "Left-Eye" Lopes. **OPPOSITE RIGHT** Sherman Hemsley. **OPPOSITE BOTTOM** Tionne "T-Boz" Watkins, Lisa "Left Eye" Lopes, and Rozonda "Chilli" Thomas were TLC.

Turning the Corner

For the billions of times that there's been an attempt to match the impact of the Supremes, aka the "girl group," Episode 699 on May 30, 1992, was one of the few times that it actually worked, with the world premiere of TLC on *Soul Train*.

To end an era defined in part by the blazing trail of female music icons, Mary J. Blige made her debut in Episode 704 on October 3, 1992, taking baby steps with "Reminisce" and "Real Love," which ultimately would blaze a trail straight to the throne.

DID THAT REALLY JUST HAPPEN?

Once in a blue moon, a questionable appearance was granted to artists who weren't traditionally singing artists, which compelled me to yell to an empty room, "Did *that* really just happen?" People like Redd Foxx, Rick Dees, Melvin Van Peebles, Sherman Hemsley, and Kim Fields made for some strange appearances. Historians always wondered how Sherman Hemsley of *The Jeffersons* got his own spot in Episode 630 on April 28, 1990. He came on to promote a legit album, complete with Vegas showgirls.

The End of the Road: Episode 734

When Don left the show, it was unexpected; the reason for his departure was unknown. Not one rumor was spread, and there wasn't a single leak from within the *Soul Train* camp. There was nothing out of the ordinary: nothing strange about his introductions or interviews or the acts he was booking. He was there one minute and gone the next. When I think about how quietly he slipped out the back door, I am most surprised to remember that there was a time unaffected by social media and 24/7 news feeds, a time when a private decision could stay private right up until the last minute. The last time I would ever watch Don wish us love, peace, and soul was June 26, 1993, which happened to be the same episode on which the Commodores debuted a curious revision of "Brick House." It's burned into my head, and not for the right reasons. As much as I wish it had been a different episode, I can't change this. It was just another episode, thrilling and uneven, unremarkable by *Soul Train* standards except for the fact that it was Don's last appearance as host. My hunch is that he wanted this to happen. If he had gone the sentimental route with a pomp-and-circumstance commemoration of his entire career, nobody would have given the new version of the show a chance. On October 23, 1993, I tuned into the show, and there was Kim Wayans as the week's host.

Don stayed on behind-the-scenes producing, directing, and writing, and he brought the show not only to the end of the decade, but into the new millennium. In my opinion, one of the most brilliant moves on Don's part was to rotate guest hosts instead of hiring a permanent replacement. By doing this he preserved his place in history and didn't impose on his viewers the pressure of feeling as if they had to embrace a new host. Guest hosts kept the show fresh, current, and spontaneous, which complemented the acts and dancers of the day. And let's face it, some people are simply irreplaceable.

The new hosts weren't the only thing different about the show. It was all different: the sign, the theme, the opening animation, the stage design, the dancers. Don had taken them all with him. And though by that point they were no longer the originals, and in some cases I wasn't even sure if I liked them, I still wanted to fight for them. But like every student enamored with his teacher, I finally admitted to myself that none of it ever really belonged to me. They were Don's to lend and therefore only Don's to take back. It was as if he was a magician, who, after his magic act, threw everything back into his bag of tricks, snapped the brass clips closed, and let the curtain fall.

I was twenty-one years old then, just one year younger than the show. I had been raised with Soul Train, grown up with Don, and now I was old enough to make a toast to him. I did not do so by raising a glass. Instead I reached for my Afro pick and tipped it.

BELOW While Don remained an integral part of *Soul Train* behind the scenes, Shemar Moore in Episode 951 on May 6, 2000, took on the role of host. **OPPOSITE** Don Cornelius on the set of *Soul Train* in 1991.

234 | SOUL TRAIN

Afterword
UNLOCKING THE TREASURE TROVE

KENARD GIBBS, PARTNER AND CEO, *SOUL TRAIN* HOLDINGS

"Don't call it a comeback. I've been here for years." LL Cool J rapped these fighting words in his 1990 manifesto "Mama Said Knock You Out." When people ask me if it's possible for *Soul Train* to make a comeback now that it's been off the air for several years, I answer, "We don't call it a comeback." *Soul Train*'s influence, historic significance, and power have persisted during the years since the last episode aired on March 25, 2006.

Soul Train was the first clear window into the world of black music and black culture. Its authenticity is what made it special. To me, the *Soul Train* library is as American as the Super Bowl, and the *Soul Train* franchise is nothing short of a rare treasure. *Soul Train*'s Don Cornelius, the African American entrepreneur, visionary, and powerhouse, inspired me to believe in my own entrepreneurial spirit. That, along with my nostalgia and gratitude for the show, ultimately led me and my partners at MadVision Entertainment, Peter Griffith and Anthony Maddoxx, to set out to acquire the entire *Soul Train* library archive—fourteen hundred hours of music television history. We were well aware that we were proposing to buy a life's work from *the* Don Cornelius. "Someone is bound to do it, so it might as well be us," we rationalized.

After nine long months of negotiation, in May 2008, my partners and I came to an agreement with Don. Although we had just finalized a lengthy business transaction that named us—along with InterMedia Partners, a New York–based private equity firm—owners of *Soul Train,* I couldn't help but share with Don my own personal connection to the show, as if sharing fond recollections of *Soul Train* would somehow make me worthy of legal ownership of it. My sentiments were most likely just the latest in a long line of tedious unsolicited gushings Don had heard over the years. Foremost a fan, though, I wanted him to know that I, too, was from Chicago and that my mother had taught many of the South Side high school kids who lined up at the Board of Trade Building where the show was filmed before anyone beyond our city limits knew of this "soul train." My mother and I watched together every day after school, and she pointed out Michelle and Gerard and Sheila and James to whom she had just assigned homework and who were now dancing their hearts out downtown. *Soul Train* embodied everything I wanted to emulate, and on this day in a boardroom with Don, my six-year-old self recited a personal prayer and closed a deal with the great man himself.

After my trip down memory lane finally came to a close, Don responded, "Wow, you really *do* know *Soul Train*."

Validation.

With great power, though, comes great responsibility. Now that the torch has been passed to my partners and me, we have a duty to share our intentions with those who rightfully feel protective of the show. "Isn't it just better to leave the show in the past?" "Why try to revive something whose day has passed?" "You're going to ruin an American treasure." "You're not Don Cornelius." And the really loaded one: "How can *Soul Train* ever be relevant today in a country led by a black president, in an age of on-demand television and self-published music, and in a culture that doesn't need to cling to a new hope as it did in the late '60s?"

Today's world *is* very different, and no doubt *Soul Train* has some hurdles to jump. First, future *Soul Train* viewers will be multigenerational and multicultural, and, thankfully, the novelty

of seeing a black person on television is behind us. As they say, however, "The more things change, the more they stay the same." So on the flipside, surprisingly, there are as few outlets for artists to expose their craft today as there were back in 1971.

The new weekly *Soul Train* we have planned will bring the performer's artistry to the forefront. Beyond making music videos, gaining YouTube obscurity, and politicking for spots on late-night talk shows, artists want to see a visceral reaction to their music from a live audience. That interplay is what made for some of the fondest memories Ahmir Thompson shares in this book and what will make *Soul Train* authentic once again. The show's format won't be exactly the same as the original series; however, *Soul Train*'s pillars will remain the same: performances by top artists, the *Soul Train* dance line, and innovative dance segments. The biggest change in the show is more of an enhancement than a change; the digital age enables us to produce a show that is the natural evolution of the entertainment experience for today's consumer. This equates to utilizing digital platforms that give people the ability to watch the show whenever they want via an Internet companion that streams 24/7. If viewers want to hear a particular performance again, they will be able to do so, and if they are intrigued by any or all of the dancers, fans will be able to connect with them through social media. From its 1971 inception, *Soul Train* has always emanated a sense of community, and now the new *Soul Train* can literally *be* a community.

We have been incredibly blessed to have Ahmir steward this book with such incredible interest and share how *Soul Train* impacted his life. All of us are driven by the genuine desire to nurture the memory of what *Soul Train* was and to ensure that its history is never forgotten while offering its many gifts to an entirely new generation.

Sure, we could just leave *Soul Train* alone, locked away, a hidden treasure trove, or we could take the risk and unlock it. Like Don, we choose risk. Nothing risked, nothing gained.

PAGES 236–237 Even though many of the Kids now surrounding Don weren't even born when he set off on his fantastic journey, they paid credence to Don's place in music history and were privileged to celebrate and thank him on his last day as host. **LEFT** Don Cornelius in 1991, before he passed the torch.

UNLOCKING THE TREASURE TROVE

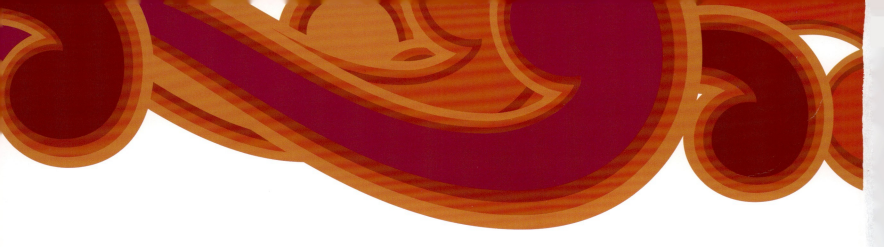

ACKNOWLEDGMENTS

I make music for a living, so when it came to navigating the world of books, I teamed up with incredible pros to help me find my way. When Kenard Gibbs, CEO/Partner of Soul Train Holdings, first suggested I write this book, it was a no-brainer to say yes. From day one, writing this book has been a labor of love. As a lifelong *Soul Train* fanatic, I will never forget the privilege and honor I felt when Kenard and his team invited me into their inner circle (and the vault).

There wouldn't be a book if it weren't for Insight Editions, which lent me its expertise for this project. Instead of asking me to stick to the most popular discussions or expected favorites, co-publisher Michael Madden enthusiastically encouraged me to give my take on what made *Soul Train* legendary, for which I am extremely thankful. Writing this book wouldn't have been half the fun it was if I didn't have that freedom. Speaking of writing, I am indebted to my writing partner, Michele Matrisciani of Bookchic LLC. She was always on the mark, knew what questions to ask, and was eager to learn and capable of processing numerous concepts at once. Michele adeptly and entertainingly interpreted and arranged my ideas for this book. She once joked that she hoped I would give a shout-out to her "awesomeness," so Michele, here goes, because you deserve it.

Enormous gratitude goes to my comrade in *Soul Train* fandom, the man who makes me look like a novice when it comes to all things *Soul Train,* Nicholas "NickFRESH" Puzo. As a personal favor to me and with no vested interest in this book—other than his wanting to see it done right—Nick sifted through hundreds of photos, identifying the most obscure moments and episodes, organizing them, and setting some facts straight. And a big thank you to the crew at SoulTrainFans.com, including Steven St. Vil, Damon Owens, LaShawn "Isis" Hardy, Rob Stiegel, and Harvey Hall.

Much appreciation to Donna Schaffer at Soul Train Holdings for being an archivist, go-to person, quality control guru, and all-around terrific asset. To Insight Editions' team—including Publisher Raoul Goff, editors Roxanna Aliaga and Kelli Fillingim, and designers Rachel Maloney and Chrissy Kwasnik—thanks for making the pages of this book sing as loudly as the performers featured on them.

My sincerest gratitude goes to HarperCollins for seeing in this book what I see and wanting older and younger generations to experience *Soul Train* once again in the form of a commemorative book.

Thank you to Team Ahmir, especially Zarah Zohlman, who not only arranged my schedule but endured its usual chaos throughout my involvement with this project.

And thanks, as always, to my family, for not eliminating *Soul Train* in my already restrictive television schedule, without whom I wouldn't be where I am today.

Dedicated to the memories of my two heroes, Sid McCoy and Don Cornelius.

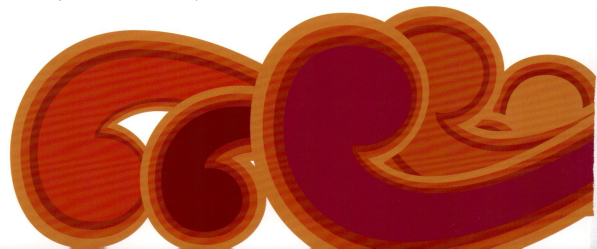